MW01224683

Riverlines

Poems of the North Saskatchewan River

by Douglas Elves

 FriesenPress

Suite 300 - 990 Fort St
Victoria, BC, V8V 3K2
Canada

www.friesenpress.com

Contact the author online at riverlines.ca.

Publication Acknowledgments

2016 Setting of the poem 'Russian Mennonites arrive at Rosthern, Saskatchewan' to choral music by Paul Suchan

2008 Broadcast recitation, by Bob Chelmik of CKUA, of a few of the Edmonton poems

2007 Use of 'Dweller by the Dark Stream' in province-wide final examinations by Saskatchewan Learning

2005 Performance on-air in the annual CBC Alberta Anthology series, and print publication by Red Deer Press, of five poems on the history of Edmonton *("Copyright © 2005 respective authors")*

1998 Publication of 'Recruits in Physical Training Outside the Prince of Wales Armouries, 1940' in *Legacy (apparently defunct)*

1997 Performance of 'I need to know you in my cloudless days' by Pro Coro with commissioned musical setting by Alan Gilliland

1995 Publication of a chapbook, "Love Song on the North Saskatchewan"

1995 Publication of 'Song of the Accountant' in *Work and Leisure*, a senior school textbook by McGraw-Hill

1992 Publication of 'Song of the Accountant' in 'Other Voices' literary periodical

1991 Publication of the poem 'The Black Swans of Gorky Park' as the winning entry of the annual Edmonton Journal Literary Contest, Short Poem category.

1984 Publication of 'Balconies' and 'This Hand' in 'They Also Write … Who Stand and Teach,' Alberta Teachers' Association

1970 Publication of 'Discoverer of the New World' in an earlier version in 'Evergreen and Gold,' University of Alberta

ISBN
978-1-5255-5105-5 (Hardcover)
978-1-5255-5106-2 (Paperback)
978-1-5255-5107-9 (eBook)

1. POETRY, CANADIAN

Distributed to the trade by The Ingram Book Company

Table of Contents

Other Poems

Very Early Poems

Invocation: Saskatchewan Glacier

Do they know where I come from?
Do they know I am here?
I the blind mind of the glacier, melting,
groping for words;
my slow tongue the sun's acolyte
thawing, releasing my song.
I recollect the soft meditation of snowfall,
the crystalline gel of ideas.
My words in rills tumble and run to the forest;
I dwell on thoughts in the eddies;
where they pool are my poems.

The legends I tell
I leach from limestone, quartzite and shale.
Mute rock dissolves on the tongue
to give voice to the choirs of coral.
Sediments mouth impressions of ferns.
Sandstone blisters into trilobites
and I laugh at their old-fashioned look.

I wink at the time of canoes and it's gone.
York boats and ferries are tongues in my cheek.
I water the billowing bison.
I funnel traversing peoples and irrigate newcomers.
Along my prairie course I wash the cheeks of rebellion,
bathe remorse with renewal.

So fall, snow: melt in the mouth and speak of a river.

Wild Horses of the Kootenay Plains

Horses are the sinews of the wind.
With muscled brown breezes gusting,
they cataract across the Kootenay Plains,
rampant from Front Range ramparts
to the foothills of glacial moraines.

Hock-knocked grasses bend with the flow
of mares imagined by ghosted stallions.

A germ of lightning
within Northern wheatgrass and hardy fescue
quickens the hooves, moves the serpentine manes.

They graze too on the annals of Asian steppe
and the tragic stories of Troy, rich in horses.

First hunted; then husbanded, harnessed and mounted,
these four-legged selves
remember the weapons and whippings,
the spears and the stirrups.

There is no beauty greater
than horses forgetting
as they course the Kootenay Plains.

The Big Horn Stoney Band and the Signing of Treaty Seven, 1877

The river surface gleams of sky
but undercurrents roll and braid.

Words are mirrors, meanings lie:
no need of broken promises
when bright assumptions fool the eye.

In the shallows the bottom beckons one to wade
but falls away, gives way to undertows of false
impressions, misapprehensions, and truth mislaid.

The Big Horn Stoney Band Returns to its Ancestral Grounds, 1931

Rivers flow where water wills them;
dams divert or slow them,
but the flood, at last, will rush again.

Marcelle receives a sweetgrass necklace

*At age 14, Marcelle Nordegg accompanied her entrepreneur
father Martin to visit the new mining town of Nordegg,
then carried on up the North Saskatchewan River, over
Pipestone Pass to Lake Louise, and then to the coast via
rail. While passing through the Kootenay Plains, they
visited with the Stoney tribe, who gave Marcelle a necklace
made of sweetgrass.*

This wreath of sweetgrass, braided,
will caress your young girl's neck
like sunlit clouds around a mountain peak.
It will glisten with glances of all who see you,
and brush tomorrow's mist across your cheek.
It will cleanse you of the stain of strong regret,
wash away the strain of weak resolve.
The twisting braid will bind wrong turns
into one true line, straight and balanced.

Wear this confidence with patience.
If it chafes your young skin
think how many bright clouds in all your life
will ride your shoulder and glisten at your cheek.

George Brewster

*Brewster homesteaded on Brewster's Flats, southwest of
Nordegg, where he raised horses and cattle and panned for
gold. His girlfriend at Banff having been sent east by her
father, George never married.*

Grasses volunteering from watered rocks
cling to the river,
bring to the broad, flat meadow
a long embrace.
This mountain shoal of junegrass
is not just fodder for horses,
can nurse a yearning for sun
that has gone beyond ridges
and left in shade a man's close-cabined memories.

Gold of the upper Saskatchewan,
shovelled and sluiced for,
can scarce provide for a man alone,
let alone wedded;
but the glint of a lost chance,
the lustre of hidden luck,
buried just under the mud,
can feed a hunger till morning.

James Hector

Kicking Horse Pass, August 29, 1858

Just like Jamie Hector who,
kicked out cold by a horse,
came to, two hours later,
at the edge of his own grave,
I've been often knocked and clocked
and, awakened by the nudge of sleep,
roused anew to explore new heights.
But unlike him,
I could not give a name to the where and wherefore.

Fishing in the coal seam
near Saunders, Alberta

*On April 30, 1949 Pat Kelly, fire boss at a coal mine near
the North Saskatchewan River at Saunders, Alberta, was
caught in a cave-in in the top pump room. Both his legs and
an ankle were broken; but although he recovered fully at an
Edmonton hospital, he was 68, so he never returned.*

Stand on the rocks and cast a line;
let the fly land mid-stream.

Cast your days in a lifeline arc,
adolescence to grave,
and let them ride as bait for your fate.

You will see the fish flash in the air,
its innocence made iridescent by surprise.

Play it in the waves of crumbling coal and reel it in.
Its firm but shuddering flesh will guide you.

The rip of hook from mouth
will knock the knees from under you.

Taut-line and Tow Rope

*In 1848 sixteen-year-old William Gladstone signed up with
a Hudson's Bay Company brigade to paddle, row and tow
from Montreal to Rocky Mountain House.*

I could drag these matters far upstream,
the tow rope slung with rain and slurping wave.
I could pull them up by shouldering the line
against the steady torrent of remorse,
the york boat chucking at the rocks
when drawn to shore by current or neglect.

At every point from Montreal was choice.
I chose to sign, to sit with ale and boasts,
old crews and new misgivings gathering;
to launch past Lachine, row up the Ottawa,
the Mattawa, the French to Georgian Bay.

Even by York Factory I could have turned away.
But no: Forts Norman, Carleton came and went,
each fort a fork for me.

When the keel grounds we have to carry,
a man's weight compounded to one's own,
backpack strapped by taut-line to the forehead.
The longer the carry, the deeper the doubt;
but there's no descent till you pass high ground.

I was too young to understand
how permanent a choice can be.
But by Fort Edmonton I knew how close I'd come
to the continental divide of dream and consequence.

On to Rocky Mountain House, by order;
up to, but not over, my point of watershed.
Just as well: obedience had blurred with choice.

The Voyageur's Oath

The author, realizing that the traditional oath, still used today on commemorative trips, is outdated and historically an excuse to partake of the rum on board the canoe, wrote a possible new oath to be taken by voyageurs.

[Oath-taker]
I swear by the sun on my back
and the rain in my eyes
to let neither rapid nor rock
undercut the alliance on board,
nor allow blister and scrape
to infect how I treat my companions;
for we are partners on water.
This water is pure.

[Oath-giver]
May the strokes of your paddle
number your days,
too many to count;
may the sun off the water
show you the ways
of tracking through troubles,
upstream and down.
Now drink from this river;
partake of this voyage together.

Blueberry Girl

*In 1927 William Sinclair was 18 when he met Clarice
Thompson, 12, near Rocky Mountain House. She had just
returned from picking blueberries. Several years later she
was working as a menial farm servant. He rescued her from
that life and they married.*

Come away my blueberry girl.
The blue of your fingers and lips,
your pockets and pail,
reminds me of rivers that run
through my forest of winter.
I dissemble and freeze on the surface,
but the deeper the current the quicker:
you are there in the blue of my veins.
Come away with your windblown hair
and your snow-chapped hands,
raw from milking the cows in the open
and washing the linen of many.
I can't pay you even this pittance of wages,
but I will hold your chapped hands to my cheek
and will stroke your hair when it blows.
I will huddle with you in the woods,
and carve a tent from the wind with the blade of my hand
while I pile the logs of my labour to shield you.
I will capture the moon and skin it
to drape a roof on our cabin,
and you will have blueberry lips until morning.
Come away.

The number of my choice

Blackfoot tipis started with a foundation of four base-poles,
against which was set a conical array of other poles; while
Cree tipis used three base-poles.

When rain would injure me, or snow slander,
I know that words' wounds heal, scab over;
with neither blood nor treaty, I become
an instant aboriginal, First National.
From my injured skin, I fashion shelter,
trim and sew it from an ancient template
to be wrapped around a cone of poles:
lodgepole pine, tamarack or poplar.
I set them by memory around an anchor,
a tri-, or quadri-pod of bark-stripped poles;
the woodland Cree use three, the prairie Blackfoot four.
You may impute my pain or ancestry
from whichever form I set the cone, but No.
Are three more stable? Four more grand?
One presents more fulcrum to the wind,
the other, funnel. What trees are near at hand?
One may be more supple, lighter, stronger,
easier to travois, carry more.
The number of my choice is like my voice;
I speak the way I spoke before I was born.
The ancestors of my memories are not
more intimate than this tight drum of dreams.
Each drop of rain reverberates three,
or four, times over: no matter; I am dry.

Raymond Scheers exchanges labour

Near Rocky Rapids, Alberta, 1933

Cutting posts by the pile for a mile of fence
around the neighbour's cows,
I pull the two-man saw
and he, in turn, draws back.

The rasp of the blade
ascends a level stair of laughter,
mocking the farming of margin, the muskeg verging.

My work is complement to his,
one relenting while the other strains,
the saw reciprocating with our wrists.

Another day he, in equal gesture as indentured gift,
shares my task of excavating water,
gouging a well from this tightfisted land.

We start by dredging slanted arcs
into conglomerate ground:
roots, clay and stones chafing the pickaxe.

One hand cradling the ankle of the haft,
the other hefting it down and back,
I carve the earth to the circumference of swing,
repeating strikes to the edge of fatigue
until my neighbour takes his turn.

We spell each other, sweating and relaxing;
but in sequence, my work not touching his,
except in what is left behind: a deeper hole.

Here too, in digging,
his work completes my effort;
makes of it a dialectic
in an unexamined land.

Drifting from Drayton Valley to Edmonton

May 1915

You don't build a raft with prow and keel,
to cleave a clean line through water.
Cut logs are aligned in a row,
lashed and crossed athwart,
layered again with more, a floor:
all four sides lead the way;
each is horizon.
Trees at the verge pan or slowly whirl,
the world in orbit around you.
When you follow the flow,
there is no bend in the river.
Hazards well up within you:
sandbars would seize your vessel,
show that time around you is rushing;
whirlpools would swallow neglect,
carry you too soon to the sea;
and dead channels deceive you,
your choice waylay you with no recourse,
no pushing the raft back upstream.
You would need to debark and start over
or stay.

Mrs. Crawford searches for a crossing

On December 1, 1939, six-year-old Marvin Crawford
found a detonator in the barn of his parents' farm near
Carnwood, Alberta. He lost his hand in the explosion. His
mother harnessed the horse and buggy and started out with
her son toward hospital in Edmonton; but the Berrymoor
ferry was out due to early-winter ice, so she had to search
downstream for an ice jam solid enough to walk over.

A child is hurt and gathered into arms
before the blame seeps in.

Ice floes scrape the river of boats.
Nothing to ferry a wingless child
across a river of neglect.
The freezing guilt gurgles at the feet,
enticing the toes with promise of numbness.
Test the solid water, sense the tension,
crunch the collecting ice;
squint at the groaning downstream
and make the choice: here or there.

Try further down, around the bend,
to find the cold crust over a dark river of doubt.

A child is hurt,
and the bleakest river crossed before he is safe.

Devon, 1949

Within the river's hook
the flow comes too from snow melt and fresh rain.
The water table gushes into gumboots.
Excavated from mud, a swimming pool
with underwater lights marking walkways:
a model town.
So much fluid hope mires the intrepid,
coaxes the rootless roughneck to settle,
the gypsy toolpush to stay.

As though water came up from the earth
in gushers like dreams and caught fire,
the flood is the future primeval
kindling a town from surveyors' stakes in the ground.

Bill Stepanko

at his custom mobile sawmill, 1930's, near Devon.

A backhand wave at the blade
to clear the splinters; the gesture deaf,
the pain mute in the whine of sawing.
The ground flecked red
and an undirected knuckle in the dust:
the residue of centuries of skill
distilled from distant fathers to sons,
local heroes to wandering ones.

But adjacent fingers will apprentice to the lost,
carry deftness forward.
That finger gone,
its grace of movement will ride with all the others
in intricate adjustment of the world.

The Ladies' Auxiliary

holds a retrospective-to-modern fashion show
in the Pagoda Restaurant, Devon, Alberta, March 1952, a
shack out back serving as dressing room.

The ladies of Devon
bestride a chasm of cold and snow
between change-room and runway,
high heels held above mud
by planks thrown down as gangway.

They step to the modern from menial gentility,
from closet or kitchen to pavilion of industry;
but flakes of jeopardy melt and smear
on the bridge, slicking the footfall,
stripping decorum from grandmothers' gowns
and slim-fit skirts for daughters.

They advance at their peril;
but decorum or none,
still step from recent to pending.

The boy on the riverbank

by the Devon golf course, 1981

Sleeves and socks of earthen paste,
he crabs from grass to waterline
dredging for discoveries.
His fingers comb the shallows
to gather golden afternoon from morning water.
Nuggets of lifelong vistas
lubricate his palms,
mud clinging to his skin like recollections.
Through the day he will sift the current of his life
for remnants of his future,
but wash them all away before he leaves.

John Cornish

Early groundskeeper at the Devon golf course, 1953,
who later returned to farming

Snow cloaks the stubble in white fallow:
no telling the crop: tilled grain or lawn?
Between the fairways dressed in linen
lift frozen geysers of leafless trees.

No trace of weeds for spring gleaning:
they stalk beneath; they beckon.

Weeds provoke a culling,
invoke the urge to nurture,
amongst indiscriminate growth,
a planned maturity.

A man can see a harvest
as the outcome of selection,
the winnowing of learned from yearned for;

can hear the farm of boyhood calling
for removal of weeds in a winter cull.

Anthony Henday

Concerned by the competition from French trading posts inland, the HBC factor at York Factory sent Henday, escorted by a small troupe of Cree traders, to seek out the Blackfoot and Assiniboine in the western prairie with a view to coaxing them to bring their furs to Hudson's Bay.

(i) late July, 1754, southeast of Nipawin, Saskatchewan

In legend layered by folded tellings
I am reported intrepid,
my reach impelled by a far horizon;
but the nudge ahead is near at hand.
Muskeg mosquitoes cloud bare skin,
prodding me on to prairie;
saskatoons of a grassland coulee
cluster to beckon my palm.
The wrist flicks to the fore on its own,
no sleight-of-hand employed.
I do not play the card of nation,
let alone the trump of empire.
When I look for the Cree, Assiniboine or Blackfoot
I am the traveler seeking companions,
partners in the trade of plains:
commerce, yes, but colloquy all the same.
At seeing the wash of sun on shallows,
or hearing thunder under the shade of bison,
our common thoughts will rise like geese from water.

(ii) December 24, 1754, atop Last Hill, near Eckville, Alberta

I climb the last hill high and close enough
to see *Asiniwachiya*, the Rocky Mountains.
At my back, the morning sun
picks out the distant peaks before me,
glowing through haze above the foothills.
Only squinting proves them more than clouds.

At last I've seen and kited words with
hunters of the woods, riders of the plains;
offered welcome if they return the visit;
but they decline, claim other plans,
profess a lack of skill in skimming rivers.

They do not hunt when I think it opportune.
They seem profligate in loss,
improvident in gain,
yet somehow to husband fortune.
They bend their time like willow for snowshoes,
back upon itself to turn direction into purpose.
They mark paths of diplomacy I cannot follow.
What they mean is hiding under words,
yet shimmering above the far horizon
as though mirage of glaciers.

(iii) March & April, 1755, downstream of today's Fort
Saskatchewan, Alberta

In the run downriver, the ice beneath us melting,
our sleds rather float than haul:
a race between thaw and escape from this country.

I would hold to my hosts' good grace
were we not parting company soon.
I sense the melt of promises,
the breakup of trust even before I leave.
The man who borrowed my hatchet
will not acknowledge the loan,
as though to hold for a time were possession.
I ask another to hold my horse
against the chance of my return.
Will he honour the loan? Will he show?

We scour the woods for birch bark and spruce
to bend into brief canoes
that will last no more than a one-way summer.
Spruce root binds the bark to gunwales
as tightly as any winter's vow can tie
a traveling man to a country wife
who holds expectations of married life.

Young John Rowand meets his bride-to-be

When out riding by himself, young trader John Rowand (1787 - 1854), later chief factor of Fort Edmonton. fell and broke his leg. Louise, a single parent Cree woman who camped near the fort, saw his horse return riderless and rode out to find him. She helped him back to the fort, nursed him, and they married.

The wind is a widow, hunting,
loping through September grasses
aching to recover April's kisses,
mellow with consent of May
and constancy of June.

She runs through the aspens,
runs through the pines,
flailing the leaves with her hair,
scoring her skin with pine-needle lines.

She topples the rider
galloping high from coulee to hill
fleeing the lips that roll on his ear,
the fingers that rifle his hair.

He falls but his leg will not lift him.

No one to hear him,
none to give aid
but the widowed wind,
who is hunting.

Johnny Grant

Grant was born in 1833 at Fort Edmonton. His mother died eighteen months later, so he was taken at age three by his father to Montreal via the annual canoe brigade and on to Trois-Rivières to be raised by his grandmother.

The push from shore,
the last man wet above the knee,
is like a mother's grin,
a sudden buoyancy and rocking.

Paddles drive through water
as hope through memories
that impel some forward motion,
but mostly swirl behind.

The young Métis who pull to Montreal
speak roughly: quick and loud;
but to a child they speak like water lapping birchbark.

Slim spruce fingers on the gunwale
bind the sprung bark to the frame,
the swelling heart to home.

These are keepsakes of a mother
who had no hand in them,
but whose fingertips are known
from low-slung branches on the forehead;
her lips from the brush of sunlight
when passing from shade to shade
close to shore.

This canoe with pointed bow and pointed stern
could carry homeward ahead or back,
no matter;
wherever home will be
the beam will splay the widest
where a small child lolls
and looks at solitary magpies in the sky.

James Hector

Fort Carlton to Fort Edmonton, 1858

Like pulled sleds arriving,
bell-ring appareling the dogs,
paws padded by a rapid yapping,
my train of thought will startle me awake
sometimes, as though I were not traveler, but host.
You lose track of passage on the trail.

Yet, when snowfall overnight
drapes every sleeping thing,
at morning you must kick through drifts
to find the dogs.
They keep silent under snow, knowing.

I might just as soon the dog-train slept.

Rossdale Requiem

Decades of dead canoemen lime this ground;
fifty years of Orkney yorkmen
lie here still with oars akimbo.
Indentured for three thousand miles,
these men bought freedom with the servitude
of those who dug them under,
their shoulders fitted to the earth by others' shovels
in these most accommodating hovels.

Their women, too, whose lives as country wives
made metropole of wilderness,
made one last gesture
to sweep the earth from underfoot.
Flood silt and willful tilling dust their own green graves.

The mind's oblivion is an alluvium,
riding over memories and settling,
covering with unmarked mud the signs of precedence.

Later residents farmed the graveyard
as though the first to furrow pristine ground.
Little did they know that buried bones
release their ghosts as mushrooms in the rain.
Women gathered them in aprons,
savouring remembrance more by tongue than mind.

A parliament of flowers will cover to forget;
but here, will fail. These roots and tendrils
are all just growth of those who went before,
making nectar from the sweat of dead canoemen.

Love Song on the North Saskatchewan

My ribs are like a york boat,
carrying a packed cargo up this river.
Trade goods of distant fashioning spread my gunnels:
articles of faith, trinkets of desire.
Casks of rum of foreign brewing weigh the keel:
one currency of self-delusion.

I have a sail,
but of little use against a northwest wind,
so I keep it packed away against the time of leaving.
My shivering skin would billow if it could;
instead, the fingering wind finds a hole
and whistles through. My heart
keeps time with the rowing
— the clean bright splashing, the greenwood creaking,
the drawing of breath and release.

You bring to me your fragmented treasures:
the furs of marten, fisher, muskrat, ermine,
lynx, beaver, wolverine
— the diversity of soft warmth astounds me--
you bring them to me
in barter for my commodities of quick, exotic dreaming.

But rum does not mask me,
nor do brass kettles divert the steady eye;
I am here to draw removable gain and secret profit.
While sleeping, my ribs align themselves as palisades,
barricading too free a trade,
too vulnerable a visitor's position.

As they skim the winter's frozen river
my ribs like ashwood runners on a sledge
accumulate the piles of ice-blocks:
I learn to use them to preserve the winter's kill,
to prolong my indecision.

My ribs become the crossbeams of a coalmine
burrowed into the giving riverbank.
From these blind sediments
I mine the brittle inklings of your memory
to light my way and warm me:
for I begin to accommodate your ways.

I learn to know the turns you take for granted,
to feel your mild surprise before my own.
Still headstrong, I drill for insight,
and when I tap your deepest memories
they rush through my high rig of ribs
with a raw wealth too sudden to encompass.
I must somehow bring a subtle chemistry to their mulling.
I stop. I settle. I sink roots.

My ribs cluster here
like birch trees in a stand of pine and spruce.
From near riverbank to far I see
blue jays glitter in the aspen leaves
and magpies career through maples.
Inland seagulls fold the seams of breezes
and all the earthen sparrows complicate the air.

Jack Chorley

*Ornamental plasterer who immigrated from Wales
to Edmonton in 1910*

Like plaster pushed through lath
he moved where it seemed obvious to go:
from the compromise of Wales
to the cold promise of "Ca-na-da"
The very variations on a rhyme
called like birdsong of childhood echo.

Cardiff to Quebec, train to Calgary,
and up as far as steam would take him,
bringing to the forest of pine and fir
his skill at molding oak leaves in plaster.
For each new resident brings new beginnings,
possibilities not tried, new entrances,
new ways to exit.

Rumours of work regaled him,
winked like morning sun on river-run,
but were gone at the glance. So Jack Chorley
moved where it seemed obvious to go:
at the lowest point of the lowest flood plain
of this Edmonton he pitched his tent
an alley's width from water.

Next door a house of brick was underway,
and so our ornamental craftsman
gave his time for pay in shoring up,
with brick, a house against the wind, the rain,
against the offing of a summer flood;

and in evenings turned his hand homeward.
Behind the tent he built his house, a shack,
a slap-board clapboard two-room mansion,
its threshold barely out of mud.

The clay just inches down,
sediment of lakes primeval, unknown,
felt between his fingertips like gypsum plaster,
the finest granules marking moments
he could have known in the laying of his life,
the silting-in of possibilities.

But with a home, a wife and child from Wales,
soon he found his trowel silting plaster
into Legislative lath. Lintels, corbels,
cornices and ceilings made legendary
by the hint of Celtic curls
or of understated Tudor rhythm.
The Legislature corridors, it was assumed,
would usher to the dome august appraisals
of the lives of men like Jack:
"steeped in high tradition, but almost unknowing,
needing guidance."

The Legislature finished, Jack continued
where it seemed obvious to go, unknowing,
downstream atop the riverbank
to mold medallions and calculate the cornices
of Hotel Macdonald, his contract complete in time
to pay for moving where it seemed obvious to go
when the river's flood brought clay and mud
through the windows of his home.

1912

Men in earth-dark fabrics glide on the land,
women in colours glimmer,
their hems in the furrows folding.
Children festoon the hayricks,
by squinted eye and outstretched knuckle surveying the
fields into grids.

They come, and wheat moves like weeds to the forest.
Trees become timbers.
Riverbed clays congeal into bricks.
Sparrow-trails and wren-runs harden into high bridges.

A high-grid riveter
fits north to south, north to south, north to south
until the black bridge closes the valley.
He scampers girder to girder in his steel-spun net,
collecting the catch of the day:
evergreen mists of morning,
flashing clouds of evening,
and high-noon grins of brotherhood among the men.

Nearby, a journeyman layer of tiles pauses.
He turns to his work behind him, the diminishing rows,
and by squinted eye and outstretched knuckle he surveys
beyond the narrowest rows,
beyond the makeshift neighbourhoods,
beyond the undulating prairie and tabling dryland,
beyond the granite outcrops and limestone ledges.
He casts the net of his mind's meridians

over ancient monuments and modern anomalies.
He pulls on the net and draws into his Edmonton palms

the vanishing point of all that has gone before:
the grubbing temples, the parabolic gutters,
the wharves, the wars,
the prayers, the prairies,
the truths and the most intricate evasions of truth;
and these are his tiles.

Dweller by the Dark Stream

*For John Walter, Edmonton pioneer york boat builder,
ferryman and mining, telegraph and lumber entrepreneur,
whose wealth was wiped out in the 1915 flood. At 65, he
was too old to start over*

I move about on this dark stream.
Every morning I unhook my vessel
for the day-long skimming,
constructing brief passages across it.
Those who take the passage
give me things to live by:
coins, creeds, and second thoughts.
At night I let the undercurrents
draw me limbs, lungs, and head below the surface.
There I come upon notions:
this will speed the passages next morning,
that will harness idle time.
I will find a use for whatever lies to hand.
I ignore the warnings of my swim,
though I dread the flood of more notions,
more things to do than can be laid hand to,
and my hand stayed.

John William Walter, 1887 – 1967

John Walter Senior built a riverboat
to bring upriver eastern freight
and rough-hewn lumber down.

On Saturdays he swept her decks
and called for courting men and women
to climb the narrow steps and hammer
the hardwood planks of the upper deck
with waltzes, fox-trot and reckless polka.

Long years later, John William Walter,
dirt-farmer son of the boat-builder father,
pried free the top-deck hardwood
to floor a large, new farmhouse.
No more log-walled, dirt-floored,
bachelor squalor now that he'd married,
now that he had someone to dance with
here on the sweat-moist, dust-caked farm.

Stanley Walter, 1889 – 1962

The second son of Edmonton pioneer york boat builder,
ferryman and mining, telegraph and lumber entrepreneur
John Walter, Stanley set out downstream to gather the
family business lumber which had floated away in the great
flood of 1915.

A father's legacy,
logged and sawn to corded lumber,
lifts in the flood of expectation.

Like foam it floats away downstream.

The son must leave to gather it,
strain oars through rolling water to gain on it,
faster than currents of father-son descent.

He squints at riverbank bush,
at full-stream flotsam,
searching for clean-cut, stackable domain.

Hidden in boiling rills and mud-flood
– there, and there – are pieces to collect
and sell at riverside, sell to whoever
will value the father's work and wealth
before it is gone,
before it can no longer be the son's.

Elephants All Over Oliver

On August 1, 1926, the elephants with a touring circus
escaped from the old CPR station on 109 Street and wan-
dered into adjacent neighbourhoods.

Despite all precautions due a Sunday,
several lumbering images broke loose.

Surfing homeward through waves of caragana,
they discovered savannahs on the August lawns
and baobab trees disfigured into spruce and maple.

This modern city responded in kind:
weekend watchmen glared, dared them closer;
policemen searched their manuals for procedure;
young couples on strolling dates gloated over
this something that was so uncalled-for;
children arrived home late,
as they do from watching gophers, dragonflies,
and elephants in the lane;
and a small, frail woman, her frame thin as elephant skin,
beat a fistful of dahlias against the flank of one
to keep it from the peonies.

But the person who clutched each renegade's wispy tail
as though he were a brother elephant,
and who led it back to corral and circus ring,
directing deceitfully from behind,
was a plain-clothes clown,
a stranger to this town.

Waiting for Wop May

*On January 2, 1929, fliers Wop May and Vic Horner took
off in an open-cockpit biplane to bring an anti-toxin to the
remote communities of Little Red River and Fort Vermilion,
stricken with an outbreak of diphtheria. The media rallied
a crowd of ten thousand Edmontonians at Blatchford Field
to greet them on their return January 6.*

In thousands we gathered in the light and the dark,
shivering to speed the heroes' return.

No one knew, in nineteen twenty-nine,
how long it took to fly
five hundred miles and back;
whether two airmen with open cockpit
could last that long at thirty-three below;
whether low-grade fuel taken on at stops
would gel or burn; nor even
whether a mission to bring
to a stricken village a cure for diphtheria
could be done in time.
But we stood there in the cold to wait
because there had to be an arm
to the bold, intrepid hand
that was these men.

Recruits in Physical Training outside the Prince of Wales Armoury, 1940

So hung with rain, this June green morning
— water pleating the air—
that vapour rebounding veils the grass.

Such young dreams as drench the uniform
seep from the earth as much as weep from clouds.

Behind swift shins and marching feet
the mist of unremembered fathers eddies upward
as though breath still too young
or sweat too fresh to foul the air.

These many young men sprint and leap
through white cross clouded grass.
Their hearts heave grandfathers' blood over
fathers' trenches.

And later sons of sons, men alone or many-gathered,
will come here in the rain
— water beating the ear—
their own lungs lunging to fill with cool, moist air

Skating at the Mac

In late December, 1946, the Orval and Edna Anderson
family stayed at the Macdonald Hotel, where six-year-old
Barbara Anderson used her sister's roller skates to traverse
the halls with permission of hotel staff.

She can trace the curves of the river
from here, skating the halls of the Mac;
she sees how the valley below twists and turns
and she rolls down the corridor this way and that.
Right foot, left roll out and back like the river.
Her rollers draw the winding line
on hardwood and carpet.
Long legs for a little girl, learning how to command,
standing in winter current with ankles through ice
and arms balancing her stride among clouds
on the mezzanine.

James Grove, 1864 – 1955

James Grove tilled the soil in dry Nebraska,
but only children grew above the crumbling ground.
So he, his wife, and boy and girl adapted:
loading past and future in a wagon,
they followed rainclouds north.
Lakes and river halted them.
The snow caressed them where they stood.
Around their pans and blankets
they constructed shelter from the rain
with logs and watered earth.
He laboured in a sawmill,
but made good money digging water wells
by hand. He poured alcohol and water
at the Commercial Hotel bar.
Raised horses, chickens, cows and pigs,
all well-fed and watered,
then harvested their wealth
to build a house for seven children.
Became secretary for the schools,
road councillor, and even
a Forty-Ninth Alberta Dragoon.

Old man Grove on a cloudy day
binds up his boots, belts up his coat
and wades through foot-deep snow.
At the bank of White Mud Creek
he stops and looks at what has grown
since he arrived so long ago.
Snowflakes thread the dogwood twigs.

They work around the contradiction in the wood,
the way it separates and moves in new directions.
They jig and spin around:
no telling what a snowflake does, or did; will do.
Until it settles for a time,
and in the spring is gone.

Train Horn

A single, brief note
from a train above the valley
bounced from blue air to me:

whether warning to kids too near,
greeting to a fellow engineer,
or formal code of railway protocol,

it spoke to me of one thing only—
how a boy of nine
in a prairie town of wheat and coal
can hear the long reach of something
travelling from sunrise to dead of night,
whether he look before him, or behind.

Endymion of Edmonton

Leaving work at midnight,
Endymion as though to drown in moonlight
moves to the river,
turns from the high, fluorescent avenue
to sink with wooden stairs
to the silted valley floor.

Hedges usher him, grasses sweep his feet
and willows bear him witness.

At bottom, on the bridge,
he slows, and stops. Midpoint.
Below the rail, the moon's reflection
beckons with a wave;
rises to him as though in flood.

He feels a kinship in the blood,
attraction to the current.
Vertigo is like a vacuum, closing on itself;
but here, without a high level bridge
the urge to tumble overwhelms not him, but water.
The humbled moon will come to him.

Closing his eyes, Endymion can see the flood,
the moon borne almost to his feet.
Its turbulence would pull the pylons down,
but he draws a train of thought across this bridge
weighted with lumps of hope on a measureless track.

He loves the moon, but will continue walking.

For the man digging through ice in search of his drowned son

Cutting through this barrier drains the arms.
Pain shreds the back.
The chilled skull grows heavy and thick;
but somewhere amid the chainsaw rasping
a man can hear his own long-forgotten laughter
layered over now,
and his own playful chatter echoing the ice-pick.

The water below is deeper than any childhood.
In its dark rush one can almost see a boyhood
growing numb.

The shining surface will deceive the lunge of man for boy,
will carry away the familiar face
the moment the hand hits water.
He will not find here the boyhood he remembers,
retrieved easily where last seen;

but someone else may catch sight of it,
carried far from here,
in a bend where sunlight breaks through
so that all can see and call the man to see
how dead the boy is now.

Five O'clock Hockey

In mauve of air and indigo of shade
the boys at five o'clock hockey
—and, once in a blue moon, a girl—
put blades to ice and rove
in clean grand lines
through canopies of floodlight.
They contrive a cold flamenco
from pirouettes of hardwood, steel, bone of elbow
and, most severe of all, rapture on the face.
They dig and slash and dig
for the small, black pit that never bruises;
but in passing rink-wide, line-to-line,
they reach an end to yearning only with a goal.

Yet more bitter, more galling
is knowing that the end is momentary,
the goal no longer a goal;
and so they stand and await the face-off.
One glances at the sky:
green radiance and blue aurora borealis
dance god-like through the deepening night;
but no one breaks attention,
for they know these lights are only
reflections from the blades of their own skates.

Figure Skater

The blades of the figure skater
glide like gulls over sea swells:
low with a slow, rare wingbeat.

They turn in a wind of watching eyes,
then leap, cupping an updraft,
and leave behind the crowd's quick heartbeat.

Fleet Feel

Early Shift at Canada Post Transportation, Edmonton

Ten large trucks at dawn
wheel headlit from the high dock,
growling urgency
among the noiseless towers.

Proud as peacocks
we trail our fans of airwash,
engines screeching
for the female of the breed: human, avian
or three-ton vehicular.

Crossing 3rd, 2nd and Jasper avenues
we rumble to the river;
one by one we plunge over the bank's brow,
disappear into the valley bowl-brimming morning fog.
The brake lights of the one ahead take us to the bridge,
for in this fleet feel our compass narrows
to the one ahead, the one ahead, the one ahead.

At bottom we cross the bridge,
the bottleneck where, side-by-side,
our fenders almost touch:
so close that, glancing aside through finger-widths of fog,
we see each other as though in mirrors.
But then we climb.
Snaking up the hill we feel the mist grow thinner.
The engines snarl at gravity,
and as we emerge into the high, clear air

the fleet begins dispersal.
First one, then a second, and another, truck turns off,
taking with it a single throb of the fleet feel
until we commune again tomorrow.

Driving Piles

Building the new Walterdale Bridge, Edmonton 2013

Broadcasting clangour upstream to the Bighorn
and downstream to The Pas,
this stand-in for a hundred men
hammers metal dentals into gums of mud.
Echoes ripple through the valley
spilling over spruce and maple
to the plain of streets and people.
No one can converse nearby,
but in maniacal Morse code
that rings from here to Madagascar,
we are hinting to the globe
how confident we are
of spanning any silent river,
of fixing concrete meaning to an unseen flow.

The way the Whitemud flows

The way the Whitemud flows,
round and back before it goes again,
plateau ravine to riverbed,
weaves trees into forest,
embroiders prairie with narrative.

Sediments compress as stories
in white mud layers of parchment,
struck stones writing with charcoal ink.

The mastodon are gone
but live here still:
squirrels mime their thoughts.

Deer glide through meanings
even archaeologists cannot retell;

beavers clear and build
from blueprints marked in mud
beneath the creek;

and heron pose remembrance
with a cursive neck, a lucid bill.

Stories must find sanctuary to be retold.
What's new cannot be known without what's old.

Bert Thomlinson's Bees

Bert Thomlinson died in a farming accident on August 15, 1917 near Clover Bar, Alberta. He had kept a few bee hives; but the bees disappeared after the accident. Beekeepers know that bees must somehow be informed of a keeper's death or be included in the grieving; otherwise the colonies may die out.

Bees lay claim to acres' essence,
distill the drunk sun's leer into honey.
In filing for common title,
they homestead in the eaves of trees,
or adopt a farmer by living in louvred hives.
They could renege, repudiate the contract;
but in buzzing through his brain
become the innuendos of awareness,
the sequins of his memories;
and he to them is harvester,
neither guest nor trespasser:
just one amongst their multitudinous ménage.
So if this farmer were to quit the hive;
were, say, to fall from height
and splay across the wagon tongue,
his neck and body shattered;
they would want to know, to be called to grieve.
They would, in myriad,
cloak the casket, grass and headstones
in a humming pall until the close,
the lowering into earth.
And they would depart assuaged,
their swarm a shroud enfolding him
as closely as the grave.

Mary McCabe McLellan

*McLellan rode the new train to homestead four miles south
of Fort Saskatchewan, 1891*

Wind without purpose
levels the gullies with snow,
just as gusts between carriages
purloined my hat in the train trip here,
whipped it from head to the ditch below;
just as the move to this rough land
snatched away my melodeon,
too heavy a keepsake to bring so far;
just as my father, when I was young,
gave me that parlour organ
to fill the hollows of grief for my mother;
just as, when my man was negligent,
I forced him to be kind; and I learned,
before the children saw, to sweep my tears
into the gullies of girl's dreams.

Marie and the Strays

Marie and Harvey Clary, near Clover Bar, 1921

Farm boys laden with rain come looking for strays,
and stay for tea.
Their words run ragtime with Marie's
while errant cows graze in the clearing
and coveralls dry at the fire.

More men come by,
riding the rails neither toward nor away,
strays lost in the woods of could-have-been;
but talk is worth a dinner from Marie
whose husband too is on the rails,
away and back, stoking the fire for hire.

On his return, she complains that,
though she offers them food,
some strays won't come:
dogs too shy for the clearing.
He explains that, coming from New York,
she knows no difference between strays and coyotes.
He is strangely relieved that she doesn't.

Love poem, unearthed

*at an archaeological dig on the riverbank at what is now
Strathcona Science Park, near Edmonton*

You are my atlatl;
at your glance I hurtle through the air,
your eyes' dart thrown back at you.
Will I bring you down?
But are you the hunted?
I bleed, the hunter with atlatl
startled by your marksman eye.

Dancing with the Toronchuks

near the river east of Redwater, 1913 – 1953

John Toronchuk dropped his eye from sky to river.
Clouds reflecting in the flow of earth
confirmed his choice of land.
Nearby he built a house of logs and water:
trees felled and squared
where an arm's reach could slake a thirst.
He cleared the bush by hand:
axe in a clean arm's arc rounding on a fall of poplars;
shovel turning earth by roll of wrist;
seed cast with a splay of fingers;
and scythe swung in recurring turns,
part-pirouettes to crop the grain.

Son William felt rhythm in the walls of logs
trimmed with downbeat mortar of clay,
and knew he too would dance.
Deft of wrist, he held each arm in a sprung arc
and played his fiddle to wring from the air
the grace of his father's work,
the melody that unsung sweat would sing.

Then in a high July he stood fishing,
shod to the knees in shallows.
With an overhead swath of his bending pole
he slung the line mid-river.

But the reflection gliding by was not of sky;
the rainbow at his knees shimmered
of oils too thick for gills.

Roughnecks now were fishing the slow,
        deep currents of earth.
They danced a breakneck tango
with spinning chains and threaded pipes,
a dance too quick to allow, unbroken,
the sheen of a mirrored sky at their feet.

Georgiana McDougall, 1851 – 1870

at Victoria Settlement, of smallpox

I came here at the end of childhood.
Saskatoons and willows hemmed
the narrow flood-plain sliding into water.
Above them, an aspen apron.
Beyond the band of cleared meadow,
a ridge aligning with the river
ran as a high flow of earth
balancing the deep flow of water.

Between river and ridge a veil of birch
fenced high from low,
vantage point from the current
that could carry me away.

The Cree girls told me that bison used to come here,
the last one seen the morning I arrived,
standing dark behind the glowing birch.
The bison come no more,
but their multitude behind my eyelids
carries me away.

I lie among aspens, but look to the birch.

The Carpenter's Act of Piety

In 1864 Rev. George McDougall contracted with a
Norwegian-born carpenter named Larsen to accompany
him to the Victoria Mission, downstream of Fort Edmonton,
in order to complete construction of the mission buildings.

Spruce frames the Reverend's home
and whipsawn poplar walls it;
these he had the skill to fell and square,
but needed me to plane and fit the floorboards,
to harvest roofline angles from the grain of wood
and summon windows
with gestures that deceive the wind.
These are just the carpenter's ablutions
before the act of furniture.

The rasp of sawing is my psalm,
carving tenons for the mortises my liturgy.
The pine table at hand's height presents the day
as work that's given or food taken.
Chairs of slender birch bent like reeds
rest the knees and brace the back.

It may be plain and rarely peopled,
but my sacrament I find
when all the few of us together
eat side-by-side and take my furniture for granted.

Maskepetoon is baptized at Victoria, 1865

Chief of the Rocky Mountain Cree, age 58

How much river is enough
to wash this ache away?

A stranger hammered to a tree
died long ago instead of me.
Now cooling water cannot staunch the pain.
The only ointment is the shame
the shaman of the white man spreads;
but the bruise it leaves grows,
like wetness in the ground,
from the rising waters of baptism.

Rough-hewn Sonnet

The 1821 amalgamation of the Hudson's Bay and
Northwest companies allowed fur traders to stop leapfrog-
ging each other in competition for good locations, and to
settle in more permanent forts; so the construction methods
changed as well.

We worked it out: posts anchored in the ground,
as in the past, were prone to sink
or splay in the wet, sand-filtered loam,
leaving laterals behind; that is, the sills and horizontals
stayed at grade, while verticals descended.
With freeze and thaw, the stress-points cracked and rotted:
the whole unstable, needing frequent repair.
Not to say that post-on-sill, the other way,
is stable. Soil subsidence can still cause cracks,
gaps between the logs that need re-filling every fall.
But we are building more than houses here:
small adjustment speaks of adaptation,
forward motion. Standing pat is fear;
doing nothing, denial of the future.

Ice Cutting

Omer Theroux and Philip Blanchette, near Duvernay,
Alberta, 1937

Snow blows like sand on the winter river.
We walk the ice with a drover's pole
to sound for thickness, ears cocked for the echo,
a brittle chipping and hidden response.

We scrape away the snow like sunlit cumulus
from frozen cloud beneath.
Young immortals, lords of the atmosphere,
we demarcate the drift of cold into summer
by plotting ice-blocks to be saved.

We carve a grid of grooves and saw the lines:
with prying, some will split ahead.
The first block frees the rest.
One won't come loose;
Philip drives the crowbar in and levers back;
then pushes, leaning into it.
With a crack the ice gives way and in he goes:
hands, head, chest and heels,
sucked under the black, bleeding current.
I lunge for his hand, pull him back
like a fish from liquid element to air.

His flesh feels to congeal to ice,
to freeze like sculptor's marble.
I shift him to the sledge
and pray forgiveness of the horses,

whipping them to gallop for the house
and fireplace, dry clothes and blankets.

Young god of the atmosphere,
he knows the bite of ice and wind
will just confirm his immortality:
like sun on powder snow,
the cold wind sparkles on the flesh.

Hutterite

Checks and floral prints abandon fashion,
yet my style accommodates the moment.
Words and pauses pleat a myriad of meanings.
Tones of voice twirl in lace profusion.
Wheat fields in the starch of morning sun
drape the mind from neck to foot in folds
that change to billows in the afternoon.
Garments of a windless evening glow
in the constant fad of everything eternal.
A stalwart cut of bearing,
a modest hang of grace
are ever in the vogue of now.
Clothes can block the sun and wind
but the mirror sees through me,
pattern notwithstanding.

The Horse Across the River

On December 5, 1794, Duncan McGillivray reported seeing
an unattended horse across the river from Fort George,
near today's Elk Point, Alberta.

Sundogs laze in the frosted air,
their glistening breath suspended still,
long after owls have glided through;
after we spied, in the far bank shade,
a horse the colour of moonlight.
A mirage, or sign, or just a horse,
alone, scenting its kind on our side.
We few, castaways in a sea of trees,
walk down to cross the frozen river,
feet edging, halting forth on ice.
The moonlight shies at our coming,
snow-trots to the woods;
but we feign retreat
and it comes edging, halting forth.
We blink into the blatant sun
and see the pale moon still,
branding into our eyelids
like memories renounced, recalled.
The beauty we saw from afar
remains, forelock to flank;
but we find the horse blind in one eye.
My own eyes water in biting air,
welling blindness in one;
but I see the sun is a callous clock,
the moon a reluctant mirror.

Alphonse Geib, 1873-1940

Geib trained as a lawyer in Luxembourg, homesteaded near Delmas, Saskatchewan. His wife never accompanied him to Canada.

Fields fall away into river shallows,
creasing the prairie cheek.
A man can apply himself here,
turn the wind into walls,
his heart to a hearth;
but if he enters alone,
his door is no threshold,
his table and bed no refuge.
Crows will follow him in
and fluster his mind,
worms undermine him,
his township neighbours discount him.
The scars of his life fall away into crow's feet,
and no one will know but the crows.

The Legend of Battleford

In First Nations legend, the hostility between the Cree and
Blackfoot nations arose from a horse race. A young man of
one nation challenged a man of the other to a horse race
on the river flats at the confluence of the Battle and North
Saskatchewan rivers, the winner to receive the loser's horse
as the prize. The challenger lost, but refused to give up his
horse; and so the two nations have conducted war ever
since. The true cause of hostilities, of course, lies elsewhere.

Where rivers join
horsemen soar on the flood-plain
as hawks over trees with sleeves of horizons.
Hind hooves leave dawn as the front gain sunset,
splashing the air into long-legged gusts.

Cree and Blackfoot brothers share the prairie
but race as rivals, hoarding the wind.
Across the finish line the air congeals in the chest
and long grass braids into fetters.
In this contest there is no consolation,
for of swift horses the slower is forfeit:
winning rides on a loss as a hawk on the wind.

So don't forfeit the bond. Ignore the finish line;
gallop right through gulping of water and feed;
ride through sleep; find rest in the rhythm;
don't stop the horses.

Carpentry Class at the Indian Industrial School

Battleford, 1895

Fell the tree;
lop the limbs for the skid through bush,
extinguishing title to ground.

With drawknife and chisel
peel the rippling bark of bison
from the blonde, raw land.

Walk the wood by eye for knots or fissures;
survey it with compassed fingers.

Plane the earth to a level field;
with a router carve drainage and roads.

Not hard to learn the choice of tool:
just think like steel, understand with a keen edge
how true the cut can be,
and the shape will emerge in the making.

Orphaned from the hearth of land like sky,
boys can learn the proper care and use of tools
from an old campaigner
versed in the rhythm of marked-off land.

An awl lays down the law,
inscribes the line to follow
in trimming waste from wanted.

Never use the indignant hammer to drive a chisel;
a mallet is more circumspect,
can gouge a mortise from giving wood
without gap or splinters
where the tenon of wood's new commerce must fit.

The rip saw severs muscle from muscle;
the crosscut, tendon from bone.

No one expects a dovetail first time tried to fit flush;
but practice will bleed the flesh into tawny wood
with a clean, tight join.

On a Slow Cart from Saskatoon

In 1903 the family of Edward Milrea, long-time organ builder at Westminster Abbey, London, journeyed by cart from Saskatoon to what would become Ruddell, Saskatchewan. The children were told to listen in late afternoon for frogs, a sign of fresh water and a place to spend the night

Tall bluestem grasses whisper, in Westminster ears,
the fugue of history: wave upon wave,
bluster and shame, repeating but never the same.

Sod walls will buttress the echo of centuries,
the closing dusk of the west vaulting the nave,
the evening diapason of frogsong thronging the streets.

Blown tendrils of needle-and-thread grass trill variations,
coulees of insight wrinkling the plain of knowledge.

Wheatgrass takes up the air,
lifting melody above the ground of convention,
tradition above the sound of footfall.

The pilgrimage to a new and ancient home
is through grasses waiting for rain.
Stop for the night where the echo slakes a thirst;
listen for frogs: the creek is the quenching refrain.

Snaring Gophers

The Agar family children, just north of Ruddell,
Saskatchewan, about 1910

Under the sundogs dialing morning
children sparrow the ground;
flitting and swirling,
unwitting of squirrels below in burrowing towns.

Becoming aware in the noonday sun
they settle soon to the earth,
young bellies bending the grass,
awaiting the shy, quick denizens
who vanish when seen.

The boys and girls by chance glance up
and see the Cree pass by on the way
for their payment per head.

The travelling sun will enchain,
train the children to snare
any chance that emerges;
but whatever the sun may later reveal,
for now, they walk to town
for their payment per tail.

Bison

Like a sea swell of untold whales,
bison undulate the parkland;
trees, here and there, spumes erupting
from lungs of an ungulate earth.
Grasses shimmer in the waves of air
before fell thunder of hooves consumes them.
I drop my hand in the current of hair and horn
and feel the flow of the herd,
the rush toward shoreline cliff
spilling bones to the shingle below.
Fleet in the wash of seasons fleeing,
these headlong swimmers bring me along,
bear me down to the brink
for the shove past the edge,
the nudge to the line of indiscriminate fire.
As we plummet to the bottom
I reach to stroke the hair of a mane,
palm the skull and cradle the muzzle,
now like brothers in the fall.

Fire

David Thompson reported First Nations practice in transporting fire from camp to camp, ca. 1787.

Breaking camp for the season,
shifting to forage further along,
the moving village breaks by task.
Some lead the laden horses,
others scout for supper.
A few marshal the children
while one or two trendsetters
plot the herd's migration
using recursive, algorithmic prediction,
based on data kept in the cloud,
consulted now and then by all
with an upturned glance.
Still, clever as these are,
while young men find the kindling,
old men carry the flame.

Joshua Wake, Quaker in the Snow

November 1904 near Borden, Saskatchewan

Hat low to shield the eyes from snow
but collar down to track the wind,
I head toward home blinded:
sky and field blur white, into one.

Boots and hooves lose sense of furrows;
I may face away and veer leeward,
but the breastbone is my constant compass;
it marks the angle of the wind
so shoulders can return the shins to true.

To wish for roads and fences to direct me
is to lean on others' compasses.
I will tack my wind myself.

The Doukhobor's Guide to Making Linen

Karilowa, Saskatchewan, 1905

Soak flax in a prairie slough.
Remove and flay dry to release the fibres.
Between finger and thumb at the wheel,
caress the strands into one.

Winding linen spins the heat of a harvested field
into a single meridian, cool to the touch
and strong when crossed by township weave.

A man and a woman caress their strands into one,
winding day over day;
weaving across with many another
binds them as fabric for draping the land.

The snap of cloth over tables and beds
covers the land, unfurls community.

Russian Mennonites arrive at Rosthern, Saskatchewan

July 21, 1923

One by one they step from train to earth
and feel the soil's assent.
Plants blossom in the chest, expelling melody.

Like flung grain,
voices disperse across the land
and germinate a cappella.
In turned soil
the seeds intone a level harmony.
Wheat stalks in the wind are vocal cords.

From this new ground grow hymns that hint at peace,
white armies only of December blizzards.

Break ground and bread will come.
Wake the grain, and choirs in the close cathedral of the
mind will sing:
there is no king but work, no god but peace.

Fred Bukowski

*CNR Section Foreman at Rosthern, Saskatchewan, 1912-
1948, who kept a splendid flower garden beside the train
station. It helped ensure that the CNR would not move him
around, station to station.*

Phlox along the station wall, or delphiniums;
white ones, bold against the clapboard
bordering the show garden.
So much to choose from.
Flowers not found among northern plains
can be ordered in by rail, just steps away.
Rainforests are at my fingertip,
tropics at my elbow;
even Andean bougainvillea is close to hand.
The furthest flowers taking root
will keep me near, bind me to this outpost;
for my own exotic mind
will be a vine amongst alyssum,
gladiolus among strange friends.

The Wheeler Brothers

Canada's Wheat King, Seager Wheeler, and his brother
Percy played different roles in refining and disseminating
Canada's finest wheat strains near Rosthern, Saskatchewan

The kernels highest under the brushing knuckle
may hint at early harvest,
the grain unscathed by cold at heel;
but close-bound heads of grain
deeper in the waves of wheat
are the ones to keep for seeding,
drying in half-filled hanging bags.

Take the best for next year,
then the best of that, year on year,
the strain refining cull by cull?

Or: stop, one perfect fall, and bag it all
for planting together in spring?
Harvest that, and plant again and sell
the full yield as final seed?

Stay with your selection, though weeding out
the volunteer and few rogue grains;
or refine by ranging through the field for gems,
heads of grain unparalleled
and multiply these few?

That the prairie cull brought brothers
to the field between two swift rivers
reminds that they converge downstream.

Thomas Cross (1828 – 1911)

In 1901, at age 73, Thomas Cross homesteaded near Rosthern, Saskatchewan.
When a young soldier, he had been bugler to Lord Raglan at the ill-fated Battle of Balaclava, the "charge of the light brigade." In Rosthern he directed the local band, returning by horse and cart several miles to his farm in a trip which often saw him drifting off to sleep. Passersby would prod his horse to continue pulling.

On the long road home
the horse halts when the reins go slack.
Sleep sounds muster to memories of youth,
calls them to stand against
the cannonade of outcomes.

But the clarion rally scatters in smoke and wind.
The riddle of no escape confounds the hand
and prods the horse to pull again.

Gabriel Dumont

I hear the clamour of poplar in the wind,
leaves competing wingbeat for wingbeat
with all the birds that sift through branches.
They combine like
undertow, current and rill in the river;
grandparents, children and kin
in the flow of treaty, Métis or non.
Even gusts and breezes braid into one
as wind crosses the plain,
as memories cross the day.
This rope is not plan of action,
not reason for being or standing.
These are just strands that do not fray;
they bind as one,
sifting hope through habit,
wingbeat for wingbeat.

Gabriel's Crossing

The ferryman answers
from fall fog on a chill dawn,
the river just cloaked from sight.
Mist unveils him
crossing from then to now,
arriving without departure,
nothing left behind.

From the far bank we hear
loons bereft, mallards beckoning;
and the faint hush of blood-rush
very near at hand.
Boots on deck resound,
the wood beneath us barking
at the rush.
By midstream the swift current
commits us to the other side,
and fog will close behind.

So clear, the hand before the face,
while the longer reach gets left behind
however much the feet resound.

Gabriel Dumont's River Lot

*Following the defeat at the battle of Batoche, Dumont
escaped into exile; but eventually returned to his river
lot. Ottawa's lack of response to the Métis request for
recognition of their river lots is what caused the Northwest
Rebellion. Some say that Macdonald was deliberately
provoking rebellion.*

A long, narrow strip of land,
waterfront into hinter,
crossing bluff and coulee,
creek and wooded stand.
Kept animals, an unkempt garden,
grain as far as the farmer's grown
accustomed to a farmer's life.
Neighbours at the riverbank,
comrades-in-arms not far
and nearby at every hand the wife
who makes a house a home.

A long and narrowing life to span,
spilling youth into the trickle of age,
crossing from blind to careful steps.
Here a warrior would stand
captured more by escape than defeat.
Accustomed as this land may seem
to the traveler now returned,
the marking of surveyed borders
is a claim on tomorrow no more,
but a pact with yesterday
to forestall what is.yet to come.

Men of Batoche

*Rosthern pioneer Peter Friesen built up a custom thresh-
ing business, with many in his crew brought in from the
Batoche settlement.*

Not them: good men goaded into standing tall
just as the blade of empire swung for them. No.
The men I mean are their sons,
gleaned by time from a nation in fallow.

Gathered in sheaves of tall but limber men
for the harvest from one swift river to the next,
they culled carloads of grain
from plains once gusting with horsemen
tied to winds of prevailing bison.

They came for more than the wages.
Kept overnight in kitchens, they slept in rows
until swept outside with bedding straw:
not less grand a ground than that for men
who were not of Batoche, in the end;
but the floor of their labour
was theirs no longer.
As they woke, they clutched at dreams
of seeking a floor,
a sill to the sky for walking through.

Lucy Maud Montgomery in Prince Albert

When only 15, in 1890, Lucy Maud Montgomery, later author of Anne of Green Gables, spent a year in Prince Albert visiting her father and step-mother. She admitted some attractions of the town and countryside, but she preferred to return to her grandparents' home in Cavendish, Prince Edward Island.

The view from the schoolroom window,
cool blue river in golden banks,
quenches a thirst for a moment.
Even the youngest eye is parched for the old,
the familiar sights from the past;
for these loom as those to come
as the flowing river mirrors the rolling sky.

The prim, pretty and clever girl was the object of many boys' (and one male teacher's) attention.

Hard not to tread on hearts
that throw themselves underfoot,
or misconstrue my courteous smile as come-hither.
Boys and men carry banners that raise their own wind,
and I just a waif in the wilderness
let the tempest blow and glance by.

Summer 1891

Ask for help across the river,
for direction to the berry field,
and it may come
if shoreline ripples curl in ringlets,
or if the curlew bobs three times.
The guardians of river marches
may also look away,
pretend they have not heard you.
It is their right.
They are not the squatters,
not the ones who demarcate the land
for sale or hire as collateral.

Spring Breakup in P.A., 1883

Merchant James Clinkskill observed spring breakup on the
North Saskatchewan River at Prince Albert in 1883.

In spring breakup
the crack and fold of ice
lifts it higher than houses.
The low-slung sun glows green
through ice floes folding, melting,
spilling winter to the shameless current below.
This is release, with liberties taken.
Even where meltwater mires the boots in the field
the yearning is higher than houses,
and shame will just trickle away.

Curling in P.A., 1885

*Many scholars believe that the Northwest Rebellion of 1885
was deliberately fomented by Ottawa in order to justify the
dispatch of the military and the extra debt required to build
the railway through the West.*

Tamarack blocks cut round, curved as rocks,
ice puddled in the field;
the curling is no less fine than home,
the game as binding.
We'll walk two weeks through cold to Fort Qu'Appelle
just to play a four from just as far away.
Our eyes mark the glide of rocks
toward the centre of the house,
not seeing watchers, trees, clouds or comers
as we sweep or stay our brooms.
Even if a rider brings alarm
of the approach of rebels,
we'll not look up until our end is done;
for we know the deft sweep and secret guidance
given the targeting rock
to justify the march of trains and arms.

Coffins

*The Cummins family, homesteading near Prince Albert
in 1903, received a visit by two men from the nearby
Indian reserve.*

When Indians come calling for coffins,
begging a box of wood sawn smooth and square
to bury a girl in, beleaguered wildling;
we honour their shy request
with both box and sheet for a shroud.

Glad of our pain for them,
our kindness clad in the giving,
we soon know that the pain of our gift
is in boxing her in, if not now then later.

Margaret Ann Isbister to her husband

*Isbister, 1880-1973, married Gilbert Bear, 1875-1972,
who as a Métis lad had been sent to the Battleford
Industrial School (page 71). They lived near Prince Albert,
Saskatchewan. This poem was composed while considering
a vocal duet, interspersing segments of each poem with
those of the other.*

Among those gathered from the wild,
corralled for taming,
for turning into menial crew,
you stood apart, anointed by
your whiter blood, your favoured home.

Carpenter, typesetter, delegate;
doors opened for you; you had built the lintels.
You now provide a roof and kind palm
above us, but I understand your guilt;
that you left the others to the wind
while you built for us a windmill.

But is not our home yours?
You can reach those close to hand,
but those beyond can feel a gesture only,
at best a nod of favour.

You are just one poplar at prairie's edge.
You cannot change the range of grass or trees.

Andrew Byrne, 1857 - 1947

*Although Byrne was not a trained veterinarian, farmers of
the Stanleyville district, east of Prince Albert, turned to him
to nurse their animals back to health from injury or illness.*

When four-hooved humans need care and cure,
sick or lame from carrying,
knowing fingers carve away their pain,
cool the flame of injury.

An all-night vigil in the barn
keeps dark oblivion away;
but the morning's mirror in the horse's eye
repels the night by its own deep light,
a brightness between kinds.

Berry Picking

Near Tisdale, Saskatchewan, 1904

Blue, bear, cherry, choke and straw,
berries promulgated by July backhand
through bush and gully, mandating harvest.
Fingers brush the fruit away
for palming into pails; but gather blind,
pell-mell until the brim is topped, pails full.
The load held apart, splayed away from legs,
near spilling from the sway of stride,
the carry home is penance.

We fall headlong to the filling
but fail to plan for the weight.
A single hand would cull the last of bounty
but risk the spoilage home.
The wide profusion of the berry
would only spill or spoil by the tyrant's hand.

River Plunge

*Mapmaker David Thompson wrote of the great thirst on
the dry plains, and the rush to the river for water.*

Awash in sun
we hunt like wolves for water.
Tongues the colour of dust,
we lick the dew-sheen, sharp-lipped grass
for the mention of moisture.

Scent of the river
whispers its name to the horses,
spurs them hard to the water.

We only just drop guns to the ground
before galloping knee-wither-muzzle-and-head
into current, water gulping us whole,
slaking its thirst for salt flesh.

We emerge, forelock and hair flicking water away,
and drink through skin more than mouths.

As water quenches throats from dust, skin from sun,
the plunge in the stream of arrival
quenches a high, dry land of departure.

Bison Crossing

Mapmaker David Thompson recorded in 1787 that his canoe brigade was often interrupted by bison crossing the North Saskatchewan River, dangerously so.

Near stars flood the night;
coyotes howl in the shallows of hills;

but this river shines by day.
Even upstream the way is clear;
I see my course beyond each bend.

Old bulls, only heads above water,
cross against my canoe's proceeding
and will not be diverted.

Others by their weight contest a laden boat;
yet with paddles in their flanks
are kept from foundering our hulls.

But these would sooner fight than turn.
Their eyes sharp as horns
ride low above dark current,
ready to capsize my birchbark bearing:
freight, head and shoulders tipped
into turbid water, down among hooves
where drowning feels like breaking ribs.
They would crush my skull and cave my cage,
but it's the blackness of their eyes that drowns.

Snow Blind

*Mapmaker David Thompson became so adept at squinting
to make astronomical observations that the ability saved
him from the snow blindness that afflicted his companions.
He led them by means of a string which they grasped.*

The sun distills your tears to sand:
you blink with a grinding pain,
blind from trying to see.

So follow me: years of squinting into heaven
have slit my sun to a sheer white line;
I can find my bearings
even in the blight of sun-bright snow.

I have queried the stars
between eyelids of doubt,
my aperture of faith,
and found that faintest starlight
can blaze a trail.

I'll string behind me this tendril of light
as a tether to guide you home.

Ice Flowers

As observed by David Thompson, 1790's

Vapours rise through ice
from the lake underneath and freeze,
crystalline fronds gaudy as rainbows.
Too bright in the sun to be stared at,
they dazzle the walker squinting askance.

Winter or spring, flowers erupt
into colours recalling
the long underfoot forgotten.
They dare the footfall to crush them.

Leonid Meteor Shower, November 1792

As observed by fur-trader, explorer and mapmaker
David Thompson

Swift embers from the night above
pelt the snow below,
shake us to still stance;
but the morning hunt for the melting
gives no sign of meteor fall.
Were these not spilled suns or hollow moons
that glowed their way dayshine down
through night's hung hood?
But dusted snow and clinging frost
hold undisturbed in the brittle cold.
What unexpected spectres fall before me
I would keep to light my way,
to kindle colloquy with wonder;
but none survives, no trace;
and I must make of night alone within me
a captured light.

Nipawin

'The place to stand and wait' in Cree. In the early fur trade, Cree families stopped at Nipawin to await the return of their young men who took furs by canoe to trade at York Factory on Hudson's Bay.

If I wait above the rapids
will you bring back treasure,
things that ease and shine?
Things younger than June leaves
or fledglings falling through them;
newer than bison calves dropped glistening
from multitudinous mothers.
Things to ease the drudgery of
nothing done but by my own raw hand.
I hear York Factory stores distraction
that you string like beads
or stitch to your heart to keep it in place.
From this giving earth we skim living skins
to trade for the means to capture more,
new things when what remains
is just a drop through rapids.
This place to stand and wait
will be my home until the treasure
reaches me as fair exchange.
I am waiting.

Philip Turnor teaches David Thompson

to use the sextant, Cumberland House, October 1789

Align the horizon to the half-reflected sun
and read the angle.
Calculate, consult the almanac,
wait an hour and repeat.
The earth will turn and show your bearing;
give you not just crossroads, but spaces.
You can find your way from anywhere;
no need to know where you have been.
Forget the sequence; just learn the points.

But lacking ocean you mimic horizon
with the sun on a pool of mercury.
Split the angle for the declination
and there you have it: make your way.

Everything has coordinates.
You start from where you are
and find the work-around.

Every step is a start,
every turn a straight line.

Thompson's River

Mapmaker David Thompson saw the North Saskatchewan
River as one waterway, including lakes, all the way to
Hudson Bay.

This river is forever,
uninterrupted to the sea;
not a transit to marsh or
Cedar Lake, Lake Winnipeg:
these are the river still.
The reaches wide or rough along the way
are part of it, continuous.

I lift the paddle over shoals
and sweep from rocks,
fixed on finding current:
slowed, but never stopped.

They say that seals loll at the sea mouth,
basking in destination;
but I will not arrive
until my own ocean beckons
this, my river.

The Hunger of Samuel Hearne

Hearne was sent inland by the Hudson's Bay Company in
the 1770's, and in 1774 built Cumberland House just above
the Saskatchewan-Manitoba border.

Will deer soon grace these woods,
or fish relinquish their liquid refuge?
Will berries embellish some creekside bush
before the wolfpack finds me?

Hunger keener than pain licks the night
and chews the morning;
but sharper still is the mute response
to the question: how long?

In this trek through drifts and muskeg,
when even relief from fasting
knots the gut,
hunger is only a stone
in the wasted barrens of doubt.

No easing the pangs but by delving,
questioning all horizons;
asking the copper corroded sky for signs,
the sleet for the rain of reflection.
The risk is of being the wolf.

The Roses of Cumberland House

Generations of voyageurs commented on the thick and heady carpet of wild roses on both banks of the river below Cumberland House, Saskatchewan; and one who noticed it in recent years was Dave Ellery, a Drayton Valley participant in the 1967 Centennial Canoe Race from Rocky Mountain House to Montreal. As he passed by he was awaiting word on the birth of a daughter, due about that time.

Wild roses wait below Cumberland House
for the voyager thirsty for news.
Bated breath hangs in the morning air
as mist among wrists and paddles.
The moisture slakes the eye
and clings to skin
in a shiver of news understood.
As buds bloom in the rising sun,
a voyager's child arrives on the river somewhere
and glistens.
A fragrance of roses.

Calling Quadrille in Cree

Trader John Linklater called the steps for the quadrille,
precursor of the square dance, at Cumberland House,
Saskatchewan, 1886. The ladies mostly spoke only Cree,
so the call had to be in Cree.

Calling the dance, four by four:
lead right and left;
balance four, swing your partners all;
balance eight and back.
Code for swings and shuffle,
tongue bending to the ears' demand.
Words that work, that find their mark,
pass from caller to dancer undeflected,
so ears that are Cree command the caller to be.

Style translates with altered custom,
but words begin just where they end.

The Tears of Apistawashish

The explorer David Thompson recorded the Cree tale of
a man who, faced with the certainty of his family starving
to death in a harsh winter, made the tragic decision to feed
them by eating his youngest child. The family survived, but
his grief drove him insane.

Snowflakes melt through skin to bone,
weeping as colourless blood.
Eyes turn in and cry seas.
There is no way to grieve for a child
given up as food for the siblings,
cry as you will for the air
to turn tears to crust.
Grief like this cannot scab.

Spit on a man for eating his own,
cast him out; but to shun him
first you must turn your eyes in.
Look through tears
for your own betrayals,
your own denials of devouring,
damning another to languish,
let alone perish, for you,
cannibal of innocence.

Other Poems

Tom Thomson and the
Art of Canoe Repair

A boat can float capsized,
keel in the wind for pushing.
Gunwales under water guide her drift.
No damage; no crack in the keel;
no boards burst through canvas
letting lake pass through.
But even watertight this craft bears patching:
no telling what can seep through weave.
One can caulk the hull by palette knife;
brush the canvas red as September maples;
seal the gunwales green as jack pine;
varnish the ribs and thwarts a golden ochre.
Thick viridian will staunch the bleeding,
cobalt blue congeal the sky around the eye.
If the pigment glues the forest in,
the eye cannot disengage from trees,
is not askance at the pond's reflection.

Trees are felled, birds fall, beavers lapse;
better to be bound by leaves,
or left for mud among the reeds.

The Poet's Manifesto

What is it that cannot now be said?
I'll say it.
Sedition so new that none would see the threat?
Let me try.
Or subtlety more precious and ephemeral
than a flash of insight which departs
before the words are found?
Let me look for them.

I will not bore you with shocking curses.
Once they were new, perhaps; not now.
I want to breed new blooms of thought,
the scent of which I hope
will linger long past experience,
will flood the mind with strange worlds
on each recurrence.

I will not bore you with what I feel is mine alone;
unless I find inside
a grain of what, I think, is yours.

I do not look for what is ludicrous in people,
for contradictions that prove them foolish.
The poet's calling is not to set himself apart,
above, but there beside, within;
if anything, as the fool himself for what we share.

You must indulge me:
I will set the stage
with as few words as will furnish my intent.
But when it's done and dark,
what will stay, I hope,
is what is gone.

New grammar

Of you and me, which is grammar? Who context?
One swims the other, like angled fish and water;
perception and thought; yearning and regret;
or, as schismatics claim, 'regret and yearning.'
You subject my predicate to censure,
for you doubt my verb. But I doubt the rules:
my drift goes deeper than mere convention.
This is anarchy without the chaos,
the harmony of a heart's unfettered syntax
found in unaccustomed syncopy.
Though mysterious, it's not obscure.
I understand, I know this idiom;
but I decline to translate, not from apprehension
of an inappropriate declension;
but, knowing how inexpressible this expression,
I choke on broken voice and turgid words
and rely on you inferring what I imply.

You'll just have to transform
this poem to glean my meaning. There you have it.

The Linewalker

Inspecting the gas line from Turner Valley to Calgary,
1930's & 40's

Larks coax the sun from under Okotoks.
It bursts and flares above Black Diamond,
spilling light and lava winds in the valley.
I walk the buried pipeline, from Sheep Creek banks
north along the trough of Turner Valley
where gargantuan gas candles rival the dawn.
I trace the line, dredged, laid and back-filled years ago
by twenty ready men throughout the sun's day-arc,
welding-flux and tar sweating from their pores.
I look for leaks, marks of faulty welds or rusting pipes.

Monday morning departure: alone,
with fifty pounds of gear and rations
to drive my boots deep in the mud of my trail.
Still chill air, but the piston syncopation
of legs, lungs and heart will run my furnace.
Strange to walk a blowing grassland as though the first,
the interloper amongst bison, antelope and coyotes.
A pheasant breaks from groundling brush,
rising on panting wings to painting sunlight.
Ground squirrels run, unaware of, just inches down,
a metal pathway, tar- and burlap-wrapped
only months or years ago, grown over.
Grass, clay, shale, limestone, pipeline:
all parallel and one. Epochs amalgamate.
Flowing gas is like another sediment

running horizontally along with me
as I move sideways in time
through my slim stratum, day and life.

I leave behind the gash in ordered time
they call Sheep Creek.
Water on boulders ripples in pebbling waves,
revealing, as clustered moments, reflections of the burn-off.

They flare this liquid sunlight from the ground
as though it were an ancient myth:
inexhaustible, inextinguishable, eternal.

The myth of men converging from the prairie,
adapting broad abilities to narrow skills,
married as much to rig machinery
— pulleys and chains, pulsating—
as to their women.

I turn to catch last sight of Turner Valley town:
houses below the rigs
like shrubs among fir and lodgepole pine,
but of slats and uprights, timbers and planks,
flat-sided, angular, storied of man's labour.

Once, his labour was the only power,
his food the fuel, his sweat the grease;
nothing came between hand and tool.

Then fire made work from wood, made wheels walk.

Interrupted wind or water's gravity
ground the flailed grain, blew the forge,
spun the wool, shuttled the weave.

Ernie Latham knew the interruption.
He came to join the crews
in nineteen twenty-five and worked full-range:
truck driver, tool dresser, Turner Valley driller.
He moved as drilling moved, camp to camp,
tar-paper shack to shack for eleven years
before he found stability: her name was Lily
and they moved to their own tar-paper shack.
Then another and another;
At last a clapboard house with cellar, water,
and no toes of breeze between the cracks.

I turn my knees to Millarville:
a thinning forest of rigs,
fewer houses, lower glow at night.

By mid-morning the track of buried pipe
has sprung my legs like sparrows,
bounding down the valley floor in easy stride.

Rock outcroppings mark the way,
show where strata comb the gusts of wind.

Imagine the strata deep in the earth
— tines of limestone, lines of shale —
damming a river of oil
that would flow like a black tornado.

Trap the oil, burn off the gas
as though its wind were endless,
man's fingers always further than his reach.

McKellar, Norman, Tourond, Richardson, Downes,
and thousands more in the tapping or trapping,
brewing or piping, the profligate sweating,
lives expended slowly or all of a sudden.

I check the valve-box at intervals
along the way: pressure high or worrisome.
A drop reveals a leak somewhere:
a geyser, a soaking of ground,
or frozen cone in winter,
a scurry home to report.

"Gentlemen: a leak –
as though our industry were not just leaks –
gas or oil is spewing the sky, the globe,
the mind's eye. I mind the pipeline,
I mind the lack of completion,
the jerry-rigged society,
where man to man or woman
ties tourniquets of afterthought
after the blood, the oil, the care, has drained.

But not just yet: some flow remains,
its destiny the metropole,
the new cosmopolis of Calgary.
Not just yet, so I continue trudging,
fording creeks and mudbanks,

head down with care of glance
and footfall like a prairie sandpiper.

Sometimes between the foothill peaks
the wind impales me from the front,
impels me from behind
as though I were a liquid flow in a pipe.

We all do that –
flow at speed if the way is marked,
no deviation possible, no leaks available
to offer questions, a way around.
Straight on – draw the fuel, mull it,
send it on and waste the rest,
like an ancient king dispatching armies
till the last one standing holds the proper flag.

I reach the half-way hut at Priddis Corner
as the modern sun descends,
drills its bright bit down to the hidden reservoir
where I too will hide in the dark
in my narrow bunk, dreaming wide,
forgetting that I am still not yet half-way.

Like night-flares the cinescope of dream
reminds me that I have been to Persia,
or could have been, an oasis of oil
appearing much the same as anywhere;
or that I've seen and heard, in Trinidad, the lilt
of how they speak of how black this gold is.

Or Pennsylvania. I remember, from before this age,
picking at the face of coal, prying loose

a furnace-hour's fuel, piece by piece,
from the guts of Appalachian hills
or the deep, dark rills of black coal curd
beneath the hills of Wales. I don't know,
but I see the men of Xinjiang Uygur
crushed in a dust-clap burst and fall of coal.

Felling trees in a Baltic forest, the axe and adze
cutting and cleaning the wood for the fire,
I think of my own small hearth and the halls of royals,
kept warm as amber by my cold labour.
I dream of tallow like a woman's flesh,
glowing from the flame she cradles.

Fear is the smoke, guilt the soot
left behind by the stifled burn,
the incomplete combustion of kindled hope.

But morning rises in my dream
and bursts at the cabin window.
A splash of cold water, coffee gulped,
and I head to the sun, just over the ridge.

As I advance through birches the birds fall silent,
yet echo still within the cave left by the dream;
they are the voices reminding me
of where I was headed,
what questions the pipeline posed.

It offers an answer, but the question is more than just:
where to? but: where from?
Is this liquid not still sunlight, its first form?
A primeval epoch evaporating into air, and gone?

Pushing through underbrush, high grass,
I am in a tundra village where even kindling
must be scouted, trekked-for,
until they bring a sun-run lean-to,
solar cells a-slant on poles
to bring the light of day to indoor night
and the sound of the south to the north on a wave.

An infold of the outcrop gives me passage,
and I am out of the trees, out in the sun.
There is a wind. It washes the cheek, waters the eye.
In the tide of tears I almost see wind turbines,

tall ships on a prairie ridge,
sails unfurled in the mountain wind,
spinning: long rush of air mass passing the prow.

The promise of voyaging,
not to a region – tropical, terrible;
but to a time where time is not draining,
but filling.

The moist earth of the path is soft,
gives way to my boot, absorbs the heel
in a decade of leaves' decay.
How far down does the trace of trees disappear,
forget itself in the darkening compost?
Drilling rig rock cores come up warm –
by degrees with greater depth –
and that alone is a heat to be harvested,
a difference to be advantaged by deft hand and mind.
Some day more men with heavy boots will work that mine.

But I digress.
This line is to be walked –
not as an end, for it is just a line –
but as a way, a long direction
to sustain the drilling for a source that cannot leak:
cannot, because the leaks become the stream.

Calgary comes into view right on time.
Now I do not resent the people there, for they are on
my mind.

End of March

I look fondly at the paw print frozen in the ground;
for though the cat passed by just yesterday,
that mark was made much earlier,
when as a child I pondered paws and mud
without a thought for thawing.

Reuben Lawrence Elves

homesteading near Vulcan, Alberta, 1907.
A poem for my grandfather, (1886 - 1956), young farmer and
teacher, then merchant and Vulcan Postmaster (1910 - 1949)

This ground breaks in long ideas.

Even the grasses wish
for wind swells of change.

I see my own desire
gleaming in the loam.
Rolling through my fingers,
it crumbles to a moist soil.
How like the world is skin.

How articulate my hand,
when everything it says
is masked in earth
and all that grows in earth.

By hand, plough and horse
I carve my first and last
will and testament.

The fruit of the furrows
I leave as long ideas
to sons and daughters
of daughters and sons.

This wide, flat land
imagines vertical lumber

framing a home and
fronting a port of trade
on the prairie shore.

Wheat for the world,
wheat in exchange for the world,
passing back and forth
in folded paper through my window,
my vertical window
to a long idea

which I leave behind.

The Black Swans of Gorky Park

The black swans of Gorky Park seem still:
no ripples ring them.
Their feathers swallow sunlight,
letting fall no drop of green or blue reflection.
Their backs, piled high with folded wings,
are dark sails trimmed to billow:
were there motive, they would move.

Children sit nearby transfixed
or lie, chest to lawn and chin to palm,
vigilant for motion.
From the children's narrow vantage the water is a mirror,
buoying swans on inverted clouds, upended trees
and compatriots hanging headlong from the other shore.

Parents watch, but from their standing vantage
they perceive the water's depth:
to them the mystery of webbed feet
is only half obscured.

All are silent yet intent:
young ones prostrate with expectation;
old ones waiting, waiting;
and the black swans of Gorky Park floating,
their long, high necks curving into midnight question marks.

*This poem won the Edmonton Journal Literary Contest,
Short Poem Category, of 1991*

Discoverer of the New World at Age 41

The endless sea had drawn him to the beach before,
had more than once blown hold of him with clouds like fists
and pulled him and a keel's-cradle of mates
below the far horizon.
Now rumours reached him of an end that starts again,
of an out-and-downward voyage that rounds upon itself
and turns escape to refuge. He called,
and men around him filled the ship.
They pushed, paddled, gained the bay, turned about
and there, bright sails unfurled with sun in tow,
the westbound ship set fire to the mists of fear.
The docks behind him sang with crowds invoking
fair winds and only highest hopes for whitecaps.
But the Discoverer could not wave or even look behind
to see them wait from their port in California.

*This version was written in 1991. An earlier version was
published in 1970 in 'Evergreen & Gold,' the U of Alberta
student yearbook.*

Culture Shock in the Year 1610

From 'Starting Over,' the author's stage play about Samuel de Champlain

At sea at last:
released from time mechanical and mercantile.

The sun and stars slew and wheel,
clouds roll and 'bergs drift.

Gulls follow, for a time,
but a barque on the ocean
marks no earthly motion:
no passage is apparent from the waves' convulsion.
Wind-light, sun-bright sails, full-bellied,
merely repeat the shining bulge of the sea.

To itself from estuaries it gathers epochs
— streams within eternity— like mercury,
swallowing all into one smooth sphere of time
that is no longer time
but only a shimmering, filling the eyes and brain.

And landfall:
headlands rear at either hand.
The island shores and riverbanks
fold lips of silt around the feet.
This great St. Lawrence reannoints me,
reacquaints me with close increments of time;
but I lose count,
I lose track of what I should be numbering.

Into the tributaries by canoe,
skirting rapids, skimming pools,
the eyes and ears take note of moments.
I pull on my paddle, raise it above and ahead;
and from its arc in the sun,
water drops in a plangent arpeggio.
Fish scales flash beneath me
in soundless harmony with prismed waves.

Behind me, my Algonkin companion
pokes me in the ribs.
"Stop dreaming," he means:
"we have places to go, things to do,
and it's already half-past one."

Etienne Brulé

From 'Starting Over,' the author's stage play about
Samuel de Champlain

Do not judge me by the side
on which I paddle my canoe:
I swing my pull from left to right
or back that I may run the stream
with prow conniving for the goal.
Straight on: though my course meander,
divert by high portage,
and halt for either a single sleep
or a season of ease and gathering,
I do not stray; I stay my course.
The map I follow is drawn in dream,
rivulet and willow marked in mind;
shore and mountain veering by memory.
My region is here, my allegiance now.

First Glimpse of the Parthenon

Seen by chance from tenemented avenues
below the Acropolis rock,
this idea carved in marble springs to mind
sparkling in the sun.

It remains, surviving the closing of eyes
through a hundred generations,
is by now a template for the eyes,
yet still startles every glance.

French cathedrals lift like eagles from the ground.
Houses cantilevered over brooks are
as stately in suspension as the very words:
   Frank
  Lloyd
Wright.

But nothing is like this.

Here there are no banquet halls,
no ovens, beds, toilets,
not even waiting rooms.
To covet this promises no ease or status:
it is not property.

I clutch at greed
by refusing to pilfer here,
by agreeing not to pocket any fragment;
for my spectacular theft
is what I carry away
each time I close my eyes,
having seen the Parthenon
again for the very first time.

Tourists Visit the Oracle of Delphi

To laugh at the clumsy-worded tourist is easy:
working turns of phrase that twist the grace of travel,
he may let on that he is host; the host, guest.

In the stone amphitheatre on Mount Parnassus
he moves to centre-stage and begins to recite.
To the topmost row of seats,
to the swallows foraging the air for insects,
to the valley spilling olive trees
down to the Gulf of Corinth
where ships of every flag pass unheard,
he intones by heart the opening to
the Constitution of the United States of America.

But do not laugh: for he is testing
not whether the acoustics, but the words, ring true.

Telemachus goes in search of his father

Ten long years of war, nine more of wandering
kept father from son, infant to man.
The younger held his tongue
while the elder was out making noise with the boys.

The son could find no words to counter
the men who spoke in his ear a father's constraints
or whispered a husband's lures to his mother.

So Telemachus gathered a crew
and sailed for word of his father.
Reports were few: hearsay and speculation;
but none would speak of the man as a son could,
and the son could not.
Rough-hewn news came from the mouth
of an old man who, in his nest or castle,
had fathered a father already:
news that Odysseus lived and was coming, still coming,
might arrive back home with Telemachus.

The father fought long away from home
and travelled long in returning,
and the son waited all his life,
till now.

Each man remains adrift until his son sets out to find him;
a man can find no voice until his father seeks to hear it.

Wild Roses on Corfu

For Dani

Among white morning-glories
these offer open palms,
a greeting I remember.
Their petals do not await my gesture,
but shake out gentle breezes from the air.

When I return to Alberta,
wild roses will again acknowledge
my perspiring face and arms;
but this time when my skin is cooled
I will remember the wild roses
on Corfu.

Tutankhamen gets his driver's license on the day of the accident

Crested each with ostrich plumes,
his two horses had just outrun their nerves:
were now at ease in cruising gallop.
They greased the air with horse-sweat,
slipping his chariot through the gold of afternoon
with plumes, manes and tails inscribing his arrival.
The wake of Nile air raked his hair and cooled him.
Best of all: the very suddenness
of passing horses, chariot and young pharaoh
disturbed the courtiers lounging on the terrace,
astonished the roadside bricklayers
— who looked up but could not bow in time—
and perhaps impressed a scribe's daughter or two.

To free a hand for waving
he wound the reins around his waist.
When he turned to face the people and the west
his vision filled not with the veering freight-cart ahead
but with a searing light.
The sun's brilliance glowed
from the fine, pale horses, the golden chariot
and from his own white linen,
and he could not have blamed the bystanders
had they thought him an immortal god.

Song of the Accountant

I count amphorae;
I keep track of jugs of olive oil, honey, grain and wine;
of spears, chariots, greaves and helmets.

I have also counted cattle, horses
and the fields that nurture them.

I've even counted people;
slaves the heady essence of whose work is in the wine;
serfs who keep their breakfasts while I their suppers, and
wage labourers who sell their grain to buy it back as supper.

I count it all and turn it into gold.
I am the original alchemist,
essayed but never equalled.
As long as I match it somewhere with a Credit,
I can Debit anything I like.
From Revenue to Asset, Asset to Equity,
the livelihood of masses rolls across my palm;
and I count them, assign them to the ledgers,
post, adjust, balance, close and summarize.

Opportunity for graft? Fraud?
Perhaps, but what I covet most
I can never embezzle:
I yearn for the giving unaware,
the rhythmic integrity of labour.
Produce and gather;
produce, refine and gather;

produce, refine, adapt and gather
simply for the joy of doing what one cannot help but do.

And so I keep accounts
on hard clay tablets, on parchment and on floppy disks.
I measure this one's work, that one's enterprise;
and should the profit fall to an interloper wielding spear
and laws,
so much the better.
To such a one I rank among the labourers giving unaware,
and share their dignity.

*Previously published in the journal 'Other Voices' and
in the McGraw-Hill textbook, Work and Leisure, edited
by Tara J Fenwick*

The Team Player: A Modern Ritual

He arrived after rain had washed the streets:
the tell-tale signs of blood were gone.

The priests discovered in him no mere visitor,
no simple prisoner of ignorance:
his purity of heart, his innocence were beauty.
They laced his hair with quetzal feathers,
bright red and brilliant green.
From behind, so that he could not see,
they anointed him with scented word of mouth.
Children clung to him like rain-wrenched petals;
young men jostled for his friendship;
old men deferred to him;
and women came to him
but could not return his love
because they knew his future.
He, unknowing, took note but did not question.
To them all, as though a team, he gave his loyalty.

But the season of rains approached again.
Still unaware, he allowed the priests
to lead him up the temple pyramid.
They pinned him to the stone
and drugged his brain with bitterness
by accusing him of weakness, treachery and pride.
They carved open his chest and ripped away his heart.
They carried it before them down the steps
and spread his blood like slander through the streets.

Over the Bering Land Bridge

As if, over night-bound northern land
had hunters never come,
arriving in this antlered continent
gladdened by the southward reach of land
and by the thrill of apocalyptic thaw
rippling peak to peak up the rocky mountain spine;

as if a hungry, weary people,
refugees of an ice age,
had never spilled like water melting from a glacial tongue
in human rivulets down sun-warmed rocks,
from scree to hanging valley to meadow and plain;

as if these early peoples,
themselves aged early by sun and wind
— skin cracked and joints inflamed
by forced-march tracking of their mammoth prey,
guts knotted by sparse or glutted eating from sporadic
kills —
as if they had never arced
like sprays of willow spears and stone-shod arrows
over mountain, prairie and furthest watershed;

had never netted herds of buffalo,
corralled from headstrong, head-run stampedes
to pour like spent salmon over blind bluffs,
their hard-hooved legs pummeling the air
as though they swam for new life to the stream of death;

as though the curling circles of trap-line routes
were, for forest peoples, unconnected to their need
but traced no more than idle wanderings,
a restless search for what the white man would, much
later, bring;
as though their generations in ancient relay
had never struck, from stone and sinew and bone,
the instruments of survival through millenia,
instruments no less inspired
for their closeness to the fingertip
than those remote from self,
those separated from the modern hand's dexterity
by leagues of science
and legions of designers, engineers
and sweat-line fabricators;
as though the European hunger for the furs,
the robes of the Americas
had not been sated by the sweat
of countless bands of hunters and canoe men
and skilled and burdened women,
clashing early over tribal trapping grounds,
then at centuries-long-last consolidating for defense;
as though no increment of progress
— no careful observation of budding and florescence,
of weather, water, the moon and stars,
had been followed by analysis or planning
— no stopping, where sun and rain allowed,
to cultivate the stubborn soil,
to net the rippling fish,
to build resistant dwellings,
to etch and sew their dreams on all that came to hand

— no sifting of abilities through the fingers of the clans
to winnow task from task, role from role,
surplus from subsistence
— no new contending for that surplus,
fingers grappling as though for one another's sweat,
skimming grit from grease, class from class,
slaves from overlords:
a division weighed with wider terror and injustice
yet also with the engine of an intermediate advance;
the grope for more, the move to trade,
the tendency to grow;
as though no increment of progress
marked off the rolling centuries of pre-Columbian America;
as though the people of this land
were not relentless in their march;
as though there were some reason
— an even small though tripping reason —
to deny acknowledgment,
to refuse their rights
to people of the Lubicon.

1989

Seven Years

I am a soldier in my seven years' war.
Confused in battle or drunk on victory,
I cannot remember how I joined:
dragooned, reprieved from prison
or willingly recruited on a honeyed afternoon.
It all just came upon me.
Then someone lined me up and called me down.
Ever since, I've twisted tendons
just to prove my flesh and bones
are not the mud and stones.
I follow plans for the long haul:
a month's provisions crush my spine
as I stumble into gullies and carry over deadfall.
Through the shading foliage I catch a glimpse
of a sunlit Indian independence. Allies or enemies,
coming or going by their own diplomacy,
they are sirens, even angels whose silent beckoning
makes my backbone ache the more.
And yet I keep my feet to the trail,
habit my only harness, uncertainty the spur.
Some soldiers were told to slash and burn
four thousand homesteads below the town.
I remember the spurts of quick, bright flame from eaves
and the spurts of quick, bright blood from scalps;
but I'm damned if I remember either attacking or defending.
I was simply there.
When did the war begin and when do the seven years' end?

Dog on the Beach

Reach and spring of fore and hind legs,
then scissored close and release:
all in a moment, again and again.

The dog at run on the beach
forgets his legs' long stride and bound
when hunting from the gnaw of hunger.
The whiff of shellfish or salmon
snaps his head like a leash
and he wheels:
spine in a sidelong arc,
legs like rimless spokes,
paws asplay and spattering.
Then: eyes usurping his nose
by glint of a gull's wing,
he turns and vaults the break of waves.
His bark is the grasp of gravity,
but the bird escapes.
So again to wet-leg, tongue-loll saunter,
neither feather nor fin in his sky-high skull
till it somersaults to his eye.

A figure appears, a woman dark before the water;
she moves in slow stroll or is still.
The dog in sand-road orbit rounds her
as though on a leash recoiling,
closing in logarithmic radius
to the centre.
She looks beyond him,

beyond the encroaching waves,
and contemplates the smallest undulation
of a molecule of water buried in the bay.
She sees through breezes to the wind.

The dog, for a second motionless
in mimicry and vigilance,
sees the seagull land.
He starts off again,
racing in full-bark armour.
Once more it escapes, rising away in a raucous arc.
Though he slavers for the gull,
he loves the bird's parabola.
He glances at the woman, then back at the bird;
and for the briefest, fleeting moment, he wonders.

I and my broken arm

I and my broken arm
went walking with my family.
My father tripped and stumbled past me
in a shambling dive.
My weak arm lunged to steady him,
but my strong arm pulled it back
to save it from further injury.

My sister and her daughters clutched him,
saved him from a face-grazing collapse:
he merely scraped his knee.
But I withdrew in agony,
my fracture wrenched by my own arms.
The pain went deep and lasted long.

When I was ten my parents bought me a telescope

Suns uncountable cascade the eye
and wash the cheek.
Near and far, all stars are here,
yet pass right through the fingers.
When a comet with somewhere to go
rips the fabric of the sky,
cool moons in esoteric turnings
mend the tear.
And I, at length, to bed:
my parents pull the cover to my chin;
when I draw it higher
and try to count the glimmerings of light
between the woven threads,
I tear the fabric.

My mind is a rainforest morning

My mind is a rainforest morning,
and you the dew.
I shouldn't wonder
that through the lazy, humid noon
my leaves and flowers luxuriate,
only to be pummeled by a downpour,
but I do, I do.

Gardeners

You saw waves of wheatfields here.
You heard of hunger on Asian islands;
of African highlands
where black hands to white teeth come empty.
You learned that bellies swell from marasmus
but are slim when full;
that those young limbs not crushed by kwashiorkor
may live on to shred from factioned bullets.

So you studied seed, nurture, harvest, trade and pricing.
You lived your winters
high among buildings budding in green-lit night,
your summers under orchard boughs.
You enumerated yields.

At home one spring you planted beans and carrots
behind your kitchen.
But with green just poking from the earth
you left for another country;
their weeds of foreign despair would need some pulling.
I came to weed your garden every week:
the tiny stalks between my fingers
resisted almost
like the memories I almost regretted having touched.

Not knowing of my visits,
your grandfather puzzled at the weedless rows.
Then he understood how right it was
to give to the larger gardens of the world
an offspring so pure of inspiration,

so clean in cultivation that behind your steps
the soil restrains the growth of weeds.

Beyond that, his only wish:
that you find a love as weedless as your garden.

On your slender shoulders

On your slender shoulders in half-light
I hang my open eyes.
An engineering marvel
that this spare frame of yours,
graced with blended strength
and spanned by tendons as articulate as lips,
bears the weight of my imagining.
I pile you higher still with remorse for things done
or not done when you were not even near,
but the mirrored muscles from neck to shoulders
neither flinch nor clench:
your blades hold their repose.

You move toward the wall to sleep.
I watch and you lead me through it.
The darker shadows become trees
and the white sheets the snowbank.
We are hiking upward.
I stay close behind,
because all our gear— everything we need—
you carry on your shoulders.

At Wilfred Owen's Elbow

The soldier at Owen's elbow could not read:
crouching in his trench he ached for sleep,
but words like bombs kept bursting.
Divining cause and circumstance
from hieroglyphs of dust splashed out in rain
and runes of light exploding through his eyelids,
he mouthed a soundless rhetoric.
Teeth to teeth, tongue to palate
and jaw in time with heart convulsing,
he prayed with no listener in mind,
unconscious even of a speaker.
The stones against his cheek marked out a rude cuneiform
and the clay his fingers clung to was his Braille:
his blind escape was immediate and wild.

Owen could have read to him
passages from Blake and Hardy, Keats and Arnold,
evoking an idyllic home and the tragic irony that held him;
in fact, he did before he, too,
stepped blindly to his own escape, immediate and wild.

But this illiterate soldier died dumb and blind,
his single script a mass of cursive maggots;
and only Owen, having honed his skill
through five thousand years of practice,
could tell us why, or whom to blame.
He could, but didn't.

Who now, a scribe well-read and practiced,
will tell us and all behind us

why and whom to blame,
so that our own escape, immediate and wild,
will not be blind?

John McCrae to His Friend

The famous poem 'In Flanders Fields' was inspired by the death in battle of McCrae's friend, artillery engineer Alexis Helmer. We have known that McCrae buried a photograph of Helmer's sweetheart with him, placed in the breast pocket. Historian Linda Granfield was intrigued by the reference and finally found the identity of that woman. Muriel Robertson, a Volunteer Aid Worker during the war, later married another Canadian military engineer who survived the war.

In quiet hours, when guns give way
to sleep or spades; when mud or clay
close upon the wretched brave
and mark with stones a faceless grave;
between your heart and soil we lay
a photograph. Though faded grey,
her smile will bloom just where we splay
your memory of her, and save
the best of you.
Take up her smiling face as though bouquet
of words between you; let it say
the fragrance that your glance once gave
her, for her days to come you waive
to him in whom she finds today
the rest of you.

This Hand

This hand, a flower, opens to the world,
takes the rain and cups the drenching sun.
On a child's head the palm can lie; curled,
the fingers through his clever hair can run.
In reaching out to greet another's reach,
my hand can speak; in conversation, learn
to grasp and build; in common labour, teach
the mind to understand, the heart to yearn.
But if the mind should clench, the heart withdraw,
and in the cause of child and labour lift
no weathered finger, nor together draw
what ready hands could stem the war-cry's drift,
then hands that profit not from peace will sever
with nuclear sword all hands from flowers forever.

Time Lines for Nelson Mandela

Decades in their jail: more than life
to half the nation locked inside their law.

Overhead the years collect
in sedimentary array:
clay and clay and clay of the same dilemma
—that delayed release will hurry freedom—
compress and harden;
and each new season blunders through the window grate
too drunk to notice.

The slow strobe of moonlight
glides through skin in single vigil
turning, month to month, its crescent blade
in flesh that still remembers woman.

To seven-count
the wait for weekly prison privileges
—petty freedoms given or withdrawn—
reverberates
with memories of freedoms with no freedom.

The day revolves:
a pebble thumbed across the palm,
dark side up and light side down,
doubt denied but work made waste;
a half-turn more and in the shade of night
are only promise of tomorrow's labour
and idle confirmation of this morning's doubt.

The hour swells in time with stomach's rolling,
acids of the analytic mind
scouring and dissolving and re-dissolving
the old regrets, the new ennui
and the constant speculations.

The minute is the manacle; the will, the wrist.
Closest of fetters,
tighter and tighter the fit of a minute's remembering
around the girth of a life's intent
as they squeeze and shrink to the second . . .

But the moment is the grain of grace.

Now—
when the only being is becoming
and the past is a glassed-in vacuum shattering endlessly—
is the time
when even sleeplessness and pain and doubt
will never, ever fracture resistance.

I need to know you in my cloudless days

I need to know you in my cloudless days,
when knees in peasant solitude caress
the slow sun's wheat, and lifted elbows graze
the brow where drops of blindness coalesce.

I need to know you in the blinding storm,
when pinwheel limbs for sullen wages work
the thieving windmill, and doubts of justice swarm
where labourers in cold-sweat legions lurk

and await their hour. I need to know you now,
as wrist and will begin to move as one
against profit's piracy, and as the brow
beads clear thoughts of struggle and battles won.

I need to know that from my labour grow
such fruits of freedom as you may come to know.

*- 1985, set to music by Alan Gilliland, 1998, and performed
by Pro Coro Choir, Edmonton*

Of all his vain regrets in counting why

Of all his vain regrets in counting why
the wheeling dust at heel knew more direction,
a truer course than he, his desperate eye
could find none leering from his own reflection,
none mocking him from routes not chosen, nor
did any emptiness of pocket swallow
heart along with hands, and through no door
of chance or power did he chafe to follow,
or so he thought. For where he found the source
of present pain, there dwelt a deeper sorrow:
the recognition that today's remorse
had cause in what would crowd his streets tomorrow:
the ache of having made turn away or fall
the eyes of passing women, sisters all.

Of all the hopes that glowed
at each new meeting

Of all the hopes that glowed at each new meeting
through her windowing eyes and ocean smile,
she felt none answered by men's glad greeting,
their bland, blind charm seeming like denial
of her need. No glance they could have given
told her to look forward to their staying.
With a turn of phrase she could have driven
them away, but found herself delaying.
One never knows what each man's hand may do.
Cup her point of elbow in his palm?
Glide his back-of-hand aside, askew
from her throat to breast? But none of this could calm
her yearning, not like a father's hand drawn down
a shy girl's head to her temple from the crown.

Balconies

—for Beirut, 1982

My balcony as a meagre cheekbone rides
above the rapid avenue. From here,
my window witnesses recurrent tides
of commerce coursing through the hemisphere.
I feel the town's composure. Eye-to-eye,
my glass confronts the vigil of another;
a wide-eyed, bright-boned balcony where lie
in sunlight a sleeping child and watchful mother.

But continents beyond her window's glare,
a far-off glimmer draws my dreaming glance:
at the flames of a falling balcony I stare
as an alien sentry posted alone in a trance,
where none keeps vigil and none but the dead can hear
a dark-haired woman's child cry out in fear.

*Published in They Also Write . . . Who Stand and Teach,
Alberta Teachers' Association, 1984.*

From Carthage to Capetown

His very footfall charred the African sand.
Flames of foretold empire licking his heels,
Aeneas on his way stepped forth on land,
and stayed. The furrows carved by his ships' keels
bore rivers through desert and forest. Flooding plains
with plunder of diamond, ivory and gold,
his men made men plough under the salted rains
of Dido's, and nations', weeping. Worldwide he sold
the pure, clear pearl of sweat from the black man's back.
The hot wind captive in smouldering Trojan sails
his helicopter gunships, in swift attack,
released as village-burning napalm gales—
and Dido dead in the grass: no time for tears,
no killing the flames for three thousand years.

Parcels at Christmas

I deliver and consign these parcels to my friends:
though we've never met,
I borrow loved attachments when I bring them.

To the young woman who fled her village in the foothills
just in time,
I bring the wish that she find here
something as reassuring
as the shoulders of her grey-blue mountains.

To the young man from across the continent
whose home rides low to the gunnels
over scarce glimmerings of cod,
I bring the hope that he will find here
undercurrents of regard which cannot be depleted.

To an aging widow,
not yet rid of raging needs,
I bring mail-order nostalgia
—intimate gifts of remembrance
from a member of the family of humankind,
paid a wage to ship her the monthly token.

To the old gentleman,
living well-groomed and clean
at the top of a crumbling tenement,
—a prison he rarely escapes,
for his hips are jerry-rigged with pins
—to him I bring the feathers torn and fallen to the pavement
from the pigeons roosting at his window.

To the woman in the long dress
that falls like slow rain along her slender frame,
I bring the reddest roses
that have ever glowed through my skin.

To the small, frail woman behind an apartment door,
her Canton lilt my only contact;
and whose feet I do not see
but whose wings I know to have been bound at birth,
I leave the thudding of my large boots
as I return to the elevator,
distant enough that she can safely unlock the door
and retrieve the parcel I have left.

To the young man who opens his rooming-house door
with a caution beyond his years,
I bring an evasive eye
and a disinterested voice;
for I can think of nothing better
to give a man whose own eye and voice
are his closest critic and furthest friend.

To the Quebecoise, the haute cuisine of her restaurant
having been too high for us, and strange,
I bring regrets at the separation,
should she move, as planned, to Montreal
to cater Asian snacks to the children of separatists.

To a family from Viet Nam,
whose faces like a candle's glow
enclose the parcel from home,
I bring my messenger's part in the conspiracy

to prove that Viet Nam
—for all the bombing, the burnings by napalm,
the deforestations, the defenestrations
through America's window of opportunity—
that Viet Nam will still be ten times more beautiful.

To the former owner of a packing plant,
purveyor of live and dead meat
—dead, sectioned and frozen
or live on ice, skating,
I bring, as quick as I can—glad to be rid of it—
a package filled with rancid fish.

To the man who meets me at the rooming-house front door,
swearing that the parcel is his, though he lacks I.D.,
and finally that, though his room is not the right one,
he once occupied the right one:
to him I bring no parcel;
but, knowing of his hunger,
and this being Christmas,
I try to cheer him with the news that this year
even the rich are eating rancid food.

To the newest residents near Giovanni Caboto Park,
I bring imaginings of ancient voyages by sea,
embarkations from Lisbon, Naples or La Rochelle.
No matter the number who've gone before,
each is a voyage of discovery;
the oldest things are new.
On debarkation every immigrant
must quarantine whatever rages in the blood
from childhood.

Though born here, though many times inoculated
against congenital dreaming,
I, too, still harbour this infirmity.
Over thresholds I pass parcels from new embarkation ports:
Macau, Sarajevo, Bucharest and Warsaw.
In return I grab my Christmas booty,
borrowed memories, a second-hand relief at leaving behind,
at long last, the hidden vestiges of feudalism.
In the late afternoon sun the snow in the park
is the colour of sea-town walls,
and the leaf-bare trees leave shadows
like sun dials, tracing through time the root and branch
of cognate languages, cognate politics, cognate lives.

To a tiny colony of Buddhist monks
now settled in a disused, clapboard Baptist church,
I bring packages of incense from the south of India.
It has a sweetness rare for winter parkland,
but the shy smile burning from the young monk's face
is more subtle.

To the military surplus store,
along with a case of imported shells
I bring my wonderment at others' wonderment
at rusted bayonets, camouflage apparel,
medals to commemorate consummate killings,
and all the guns:
the strangely dignified ones the Great War rifles
carried by whole cities of men
like lemmings to the trenches.
Now sons follow fathers

wandering through these stacks of weapons,
boys frantic with excitement,
men glazed with contentment.

To a small boy I bring a parcel
large enough to be a father,
though I see from disused labels
that the packing case once held rifles.

To a little girl I bring a parcel
large enough to be a sister.
I walk away and lose the girl's delight,
I lose the sister, I lose a daughter.

To the doctor's wife
whom I chime from an afternoon shower,
her boredom and bemused awareness
steaming through her bathrobe
while I fumble with the signing form and payment
—for hers is a parcel expected, ordered and invoiced—
to her I bring another, involuntary gift:
one she sees through.
Though I busy myself with paper work and don't look up,
I know that her eyes are thanking me.

To the angry man I work with,
who returned —from a year of erudition brewed at univer-
sity— to this menial delivery,
I bring my every missort,
all the parcels misdirected from their destinations,
their presumed addresses more exclusive
and suburban than any he and I frequent.

Very Early Poems

I See Myself

I see myself a soldier, tall and straight,
parading through an embarkation street
in patriotic frenzy, through crowds that seethe
with pride at watching every living scythe
proceed in lock-step toward the field
where ripened seed and farmer both are felled.
Like children's men of tin we go when called
to table-top or floor, to kill or be killed.
Such pliant toys for playful little boys!

I see myself a soldier, face intent,
polishing the metal's bluish tint
to awe the enemy with Heaven's light,
a halo calling men who flinch too late
before the fall of Our omniscient feet,
rewarding them for lack of fear with Fate;
I see the rifle, bayonet, grenades,
and all the tools that God's apprentice needs.
Such useful toys for serious little boys!

I see myself a soldier, wet and cold,
waiting as a sentry to be called
to sunset watch, when forms of men begin
to lose distinction, falling back again
through flashing scarlet to oblivion.
When sinking down as war's alluvium
we wonder if the night and soothing winds
are really only "Self-inflicted Wounds."
Such engaging toys for idle little boys!

I see myself a soldier, laid out and still,
flesh freshly starched and in the current style;
for men with whom I marched in smart array
were summer-clad, and winter turned awry
their wretched honour, and they took my gear,
though leaving me my snow-enswaddled gore.
Me and other clumps they count and haul
to keep them warm until they find a hole.
Such comforting toys for anxious little boys!

I see myself a soldier, flat and level,
a stratum of the soil, but wise and civil;
now a gardener, I trigger shoots
with fingers that remember firing shots
no less haphazardly toward the fray;
where each in sudden crimson blossoms free;
where at my coaxing each wild flower rises,
reckless poppies mixed with ardent roses.
Such redemptive toys for lonely little boys!

- early 1970's

In the Craft of Genesis

Adam, pour the sweet, red wine
and Eve, break the risen bread;
but then let Cain, my dinner guest
and I do all the rest.

- 1969

APRYLLIS

The first engendered root enwombed the word;
that April spillage pierced the aphonic earth
to plunge and to ply against the marching sun
blew ice-white surd into verb, dry tuber to lung.
The stalk that April's paradox cajoled
sprang quick with etymon to greenery's brogue,
spread quietly the runic leaf and twig
to foliate acrostically the wind
and whistled, gaily (pipe to the winding prologue,
teller of earthy tales), the pilgrim's homage,
proffered as the frail and flowering shrine
to Life, the lonely wistful martyr of Time.
The bloom that first forgot to wonder why
and winter's what, when drunk with April wine,
did not dangle on the verb to be,
but fused its idiom's own emergency
within its morning mouthing crucible,
stamen-tongued, petal-palated,
and pistil-voiced. From the legendary sun
and rumoured earth the yellow flower culled
in uttered alchemy the golden timbre
of eugenic blossoms teeming, singing
a-breath with breezes blown from hillside chorus
to choir'd pond, from buttercup to lotus.
The flower first left mute by autumn's cadence
(heralded by the trumpeting shoots of April)
had yet the last word— the seed evoking

spring's jig-roundelay, the word imploring
Dance the rain-dance, sing songs to the sun until birth:
The last engendered root emwombs the word.

- 1969

Like the Lion Caged

Like the lion caged
the poet sits and, bloody-eyed,
decries the eyes beyond the bars.
From refuge in the darkest,
most confining corners of his cage,
he glares, too angry to be mad.
Like the lion staged,
the poet now and then endeavours
to intimidate the crowd
with leaping threats and warning roars
at those who gape but never flinch—
for they have caged the lion's rage.
Like the lion waged
in private war, the poet paces
circles in his narrow cell,
and sometimes tries the bars that wall
the laughing people from his quaking
terror of a captive death.

- 1969

Ballade à François Villon

- 1970

Quand vers l'hiver je me sens chassé,
dépeché, dépaigné, la voile au vent,
et mon coeur vers l'année qui vient de passer
se tourne et tombe y en parcourant;
quand l'hâte des feuilles me rappelle du printemps,
saison sans cesse qui rien ne prevoit,
je pense aux autres sous le vent d'antan,
et je ne peux pas dire adieu, François.

Quand en septembre l'avril se fracasse
par terre et se trouve de nouveau poisson*,
mon coeur recourt, se débarrasse
des bruits du vent de cette saison,
et entend une autre, l'ancienne chanson
dont l'air est l'esprit écrit de toi,
dont l'harmonie nous partageons;
et je ne peux pas dire adieu, François.

D'alors, à l'auberge, je suis des votres
quand tes vers aux brises du Quartier tu pends;
Marc-Aurèle à la main, Marion à l'autre,
le vin en veine et le coeur craquant,
tu sais saisir les vents de temps,
tu sais me montrer l'âme comme elle soit:
voleur-élève, je prends, j'apprends,
et je ne peux dire adieu, François.

Quand j'écoute l'automne, j'entends
(jusqu'à la fonte des neiges sans voix)
les paroles que tu me laisse sur le vent,
et je ne peux pas dire adieu, François.

   * *poisson d'avril* = *april fool*

Printed in Canada